Surviving and Thriving

*How to Ensure Your First Year at Work
Doesn't End in Disaster*

Rae A. Stonehouse

Live For Excellence Productions

Copyright

ISBN - E-book: 978-1-998813-20-9

ISBN – Paperback: 978-1-998813-21-6

ISBN – Audiobook: 978-1-998813-22-3

Introduction

Starting your first job can be an exciting and nerve-racking experience. You're eager to make a good impression and prove yourself to your new colleagues and employer. But before you dive headfirst into your new role, there is one important factor to remember: workplace safety.

Occupational health and safety (OH&S) should be a top priority for any workplace, despite industry or sector. Proper training and equipment, along with a focus on risk prevention, can help prevent accidents, injuries, and fatalities on the job. As a new employee, it's your responsibility to understand and follow the safety protocols set by your employer.

Here are some startling statistics:

- In 2020, there were about **17.3 million workers under the age of 25**. These workers represented **11.7%** of the total workforce.

- In 2020, **352 workers under the age of 25 died** from work-related injuries. Among these deaths were **29 young workers aged 15 to 24**.
- In 2020, the incidence rate for non-fatal injuries for workers, ages 16–19, was **149.8 per 10,000 full-time employees (FTE)** and **141.8 per 10,000 FTE** for workers, ages 20–24.

According to SafeThink, among injured workers under the age of 25, over 50% of them were hurt in the first six months on the job. Nearly 20% of the injuries and fatalities happen during the first month on the job.

In 2020, the rate of work-related injuries treated in emergency departments for workers, ages 15–24, was **1.5 times greater** than the rate for workers 25 years of age and older.

According to the National Institute for Occupational Safety and Health (NIOSH), young workers (ages 15-24) are twice as likely to be injured on the job as older workers. This is largely due to their lack of experience, training, and maturity. In addition, young workers may not be aware of their rights and responsibilities under workplace safety laws and regulations.

In the United States, an average of 358 young workers die each year from work-related injuries, according to the Bureau of Labor Statistics. The most common causes of these fatalities include transportation incidents, slips, trips, and falls, and contact with objects and equipment.

In addition to the risk of fatal injuries, young workers are also at risk of non-fatal injuries that can have long-term consequences for their health and well-being. For example, young workers may be more likely to experience musculoskeletal injuries due to their physical immaturity and lack of conditioning.

Certain industries and occupations pose a higher risk of injury and fatality for young workers. For example, young workers in the construction, agriculture, and manufacturing industries are more likely to be injured on the job than those in other industries. Similarly, young workers in occupations that involve driving or operating heavy machinery are at higher risk of transportation-related injuries.

This book helps you navigate the world of workplace safety as you start your career. We'll explore the most common hazards you may encounter on the job and provide practical tips for staying safe and healthy in the workplace. Whether you're working in an office, a factory, or a construction site, this guide will equip you with the knowledge you need to succeed.

- In these chapters, we'll cover topics such as:
- Understanding your employer's OH&S policy
- Identifying and reporting hazards in the workplace
- Using personal protective equipment (PPE) correctly
- Preventing common injuries, such as strains and sprains
- Dealing with emergencies, such as fires and medical incidents
- Promoting mental health and well-being in the workplace

And much more!

According to the National Institute for Occupational Safety and Health (NIOSH), young workers have high rates of job-related injury. These injuries are often the result of the many hazards present in the places they typically work, such as sharp knives and slippery floors in restaurants. Limited or no prior work experience and a lack of safety training also contribute to high injury rates.

It's important for young people to be aware of these risks and take necessary precautions while working.

By following the tips and advice in this book, you can start your job with confidence, knowing that you're doing everything possible to stay safe and healthy on the job. Remember, workplace safety isn't just important – it's essential. Let's get started!

But before we do, it's probably a good idea for me to explain who I am and why I wrote this book.

I am a recently retired registered nurse having worked for over four decades in psychiatry/mental health. For most of that time I was actively involved in Occupational Health & Safety in my worksites as a worker representative for three trade unions. I served as a Cochair on my worksite's JOSH (Joint Occupational Health & Safety Committee).

As a JOSH Committee Cochair I was involved in accident investigation, conducting workplace safety inspections, implementing workplace and wellness programs, and developing policies and procedures.

Working in healthcare exposes the worker to much of the same safety hazards as other industries perhaps with the exception of manufacturing.

As the field of Occupational Health & Safety has evolved, workers are gaining more protection from safety hazards in their worksites and the ability to solve problems backed by legislation. At the same time, Employers also have responsibilities to provide a safe work environment also enforced by legislation.

I started my career long before health and safety issues were being addressed. My first job, before I was in nursing, was working in the Dietary Department in a large community psychiatric hospital.

At the time, I wanted to be a chef and working in a large kitchen seemed to be a good way to enter the field.

As a Porter i.e., Dietary Assistant, I was responsible for all parts of helping the cooks and the chef in preparing meals for close to 400 patients. Many of my duties had risk involved. For example, one day I had to unload a truck of 100, 75-pound bags of potatoes and load them into a walk-in refrigerator. The next day, I had another 35 bags to unload. My back ached for weeks.

On another occasion I recall prying the lid off an 8 ½ gallon stainless steel soup container. All my fingers came in contact with the rim of the container causing me severe pain and to black out. As I was lying on the floor, I recall one cook discovering me and yelling "help, there is a dead man back here!" I was lucky though as when I was collaps-ing, I had missed some very hot ovens.

My plan to become a chef went sideways. I went from food prepara-tion, to running the dishwasher and then on to operating the pot washer.

At one point I was transferred to work at a nearby maximum-security hospital for the criminally insane in the Dietary Department. Here I worked alongside murderers, kidnappers and basically perpetrators of any heinous crimes you could imagine. I was 19 years old. There was no training or preparation for my role and duties. I spent my days working alongside these criminals.

I recall my first day there being introduced to the dietary crew. There was one young fellow named Bobby. Bobby was holding a 12-inch butchers' knife and chopping vegetables on a carving board. He says, "do you know why I'm here?" To which I replied "No."

Bobby replied "I killed my father with a knife just like this. You look a lot like my father."

As my career opportunities within the Dietary Department and my aspirations to become a chef were thwarted, I looked elsewhere and enrolled in nursing training.

Working over four decades in healthcare I experienced many critical incidents and safety hazards but those are beyond the scope of this book as they were beyond our framework i.e., your first year at work.

I've wanted to write this book for a long time. I shudder every time I read or hear about an accident that has taken a young worker's life or livelihood.

This book is focused on Occupational Health & Safety for young workers starting a new job. The saying "what you don't know can hurt you" holds true.

While the field of Occupational Health & Safety is improving, you will find many employers don't care, don't know about OH&S matters or who actively ignore regulations in favor of increased profit. OH&S legislation is in place to deal with those employers. Worker's Compensation boards are gaining more authority and clout in many jurisdictions and have been levying hefty fines for employers who don't comply.

This book isn't written to be read linearly i.e., from front to back. As in my other personal/professional self-development books I use what I call an 'onion' method. I explore a topic in depth and often peel back a layer and revisit a topic from a different perspective.

Introduction

My hope is you have the opportunity to read this book in advance and refer to it often as you progress through your first year working.

Onwards and upwards!

Rae A. Stonehouse,
Author
April 2023

Chapter 1

A Safe Start To Your First Job

Whether you're working in an office, warehouse, or construction site, there are always risks involved. In this chapter, we'll go over some basic Occupational Health and Safety (OH&S) tips to help you stay safe and healthy on the job.

Know Your Rights:

As an employee, you have the right to a safe workplace. This means that your employer is responsible for providing you with the training, equipment, and procedures to keep you safe. It's also your responsibility to follow these protocols and report any hazards or incidents you come across.

Follow Proper Procedures:

Every workplace has its own set of procedures and protocols to follow. Before starting your job, understand your employer's OH&S policy.

. . .

Whether it's wearing personal protective equipment (PPE), using machinery, or handling hazardous materials, it's important to follow these procedures carefully. Don't take shortcuts or ignore safety guidelines, even if you're in a hurry or think it's unnecessary. If you have any questions, please ask your supervisor or Human Resources (HR) representative.

Report Hazards and Incidents:

If you notice any hazards or potential safety risks in your workplace, report them to your supervisor immediately. This could include things like faulty equipment, unsafe work practices, or hazardous materials. If you're involved in an incident or accident, report it and seek medical attention if necessary.

Take Care of Yourself:

In addition to following proper safety procedures, it's important to take care of your physical and mental health. This could include things like getting enough sleep, eating a healthy diet, and taking breaks when you need them. Don't hesitate to speak to your employer or HR department if you need support or accommodations to help you stay healthy and safe on the job.

One of the most important things you can do to stay safe on the job is to be aware of your surroundings and identify any potential hazards. This could include things like slippery floors, exposed wires, or improperly stored chemicals. If you notice any hazards or potential safety risks, report them to your supervisor immediately.

Use Personal Protective Equipment (PPE) Correctly:

PPE, such as safety glasses, hard hats, and gloves, can help protect you from workplace hazards. It's important to use PPE correctly and to make sure it's in good condition before using it. If you're unsure about how to use PPE, ask your supervisor or a coworker for guidance.

Prevent Common Injuries:

Common workplace injuries, such as strains and sprains, can often be prevented by using proper lifting techniques, taking breaks, and using ergonomic equipment. Make sure you're aware of the risks associated with your job and try to prevent injury.

Deal with Emergencies:

Knowing how to deal with emergencies, such as fires or medical incidents, is crucial for staying safe on the job. Make sure you're familiar with your workplace's emergency procedures and know where to find first aid kits and fire extinguishers.

* * *

In our next chapter we introduce workplace safety.

Chapter 2

Introduction To Workplace Safety

A Brief History of Workplace Safety Regulations and Their Significance in Protecting Employees:

Over the last two centuries, workplace safety regulations have evolved and become more stringent to protect employees. During the Industrial Revolution in the mid-1800s, unsafe working conditions were rampant, and workers were often injured or killed on the job. However, it was not until 1864 that the first workplace safety law was enacted in the UK, known as the Factory Act. This law required employers to provide proper ventilation, fencing around dangerous machinery, and clean drinking water to workers.

In the early 1900s, workplace safety regulations became more prevalent in the U.S. as well. In 1911, the Triangle Shirtwaist Factory in New York City caught on fire, killing 146 workers. This tragedy helped to form the U.S. Department of Labor and the enactment of the Occupational Safety and Health Act of 1970, which established the Occupational Safety and Health Administration (OSHA).

OSHA sets and enforces safety standards for workplaces, conducts inspections, and provides education and training for employers and employees on a variety of safety topics. The agency has played a significant role in reducing workplace injuries and fatalities over the years. In the 1970s, the number of workplace deaths in the U.S. was around 14,000 per year. By 2019, that number had dropped to around 5,000 per year.

Workplace safety regulations are significant in protecting employees because they make sure employers provide safe working conditions and equipment, train employees on how to work safely, and investigate accidents and injuries to prevent them from happening again. These regulations also protect employees from retaliation if they report unsafe conditions or refuse to work in dangerous situations. Overall, workplace safety regulations are essential for preventing injuries, illnesses, and deaths on the job and creating a safer and healthier workforce.

The Role of Employers in Establishing A Safe Work Environment And Their Legal Obligations In Maintaining Workplace Safety:

Employers play a crucial role in establishing a safe work environment for their employees. It is their responsibility to provide a hazard-free workplace, implement safety measures, and train their employees on workplace safety procedures. In addition, employers have legal obligations to maintain workplace safety to prevent accidents and injuries.

. . .

The Occupational Safety and Health Administration (OSHA) sets standards for workplace safety, and employers must comply with these standards. This includes providing personal protective equipment, implementing safety programs, and providing a hazard communication program. Employers must also conduct regular inspections to identify and mitigate workplace hazards.

Employers also must report workplace accidents and injuries to OSHA and keep detailed records of incidents that occur in the workplace. They must investigate accidents to identify the cause and take corrective action to prevent future incidents from occurring.

Employers play a crucial role in maintaining workplace safety by implementing safety measures, providing training, and complying with legal regulations. By focusing on workplace safety, employers can reduce accidents, injuries, and illnesses, and create a safer and healthier workplace for their employees.

An Overview of Government Agencies Responsible for Enforcing Workplace Safety Regulations, Such as OSHA In The U.S.:

In the United States, the Occupational Safety and Health Administration (OSHA) is the primary federal agency responsible for enforcing workplace safety regulations. OSHA was created in 1970 as part of the Occupational Safety and Health Act, which requires employers to provide a workplace free of recognized hazards that can cause death or serious injury.

OSHA sets and enforces workplace safety standards, provides training and education to workers and employers, and conducts inspections and investigations to ensure compliance with regulations. Employers found to violate OSHA regulations can face penalties, fines, and enforcement actions, such as citations and orders to correct hazards.

In addition to OSHA, there are also state agencies responsible for enforcing workplace safety regulations. These agencies may adopt OSHA standards or have their own, more stringent regulations in place. Employers must follow both federal and state regulations, whichever are more protective of workers.

Other government agencies with a role in enforcing workplace safety regulations include the Environmental Protection Agency (EPA), which regulates hazardous materials and pollutants that can be present in workplaces, and the Mine Safety and Health Administration (MSHA), which enforces safety and health standards in mines and other related industries.

Overall, these government agencies play a crucial role in protecting workers from occupational hazards and making sure employers provide a safe and healthy workplace.

The Importance of Employee Training and Education in Identifying And Avoiding Workplace Hazards:

Employee training and education are vital in identifying and avoiding workplace hazards. Proper training and education help employees understand the risks involved in their work and the measures they need to take to reduce those risks.

. . .

A well-informed and well-trained workforce is better equipped to identify workplace hazards and adopt safe work practices. When employees are trained on how to identify and report hazards, they can help to prevent accidents and injuries in the workplace.

Also, employee training and education provide employees with the knowledge and skills they need to run equipment safely and use personal protective equipment (PPE) correctly. This reduces the risk of serious accidents and injuries happening when employees are operating equipment or working in hazardous environments.

An organization that invests in employee training and education is likely to have fewer workplace accidents and injuries. This reduces absenteeism and increases productivity, leading to better business outcomes.

Employee training and education are essential to effectively identify and avoid workplace hazards. Employers should develop robust training and educational programs to improve the safety of their workforce and promote a positive safety culture in their organization.

The Potential Risks and Hazards in Various Types of Workplaces, Such As Factories, Construction Sites & Offices:

Different workplaces pose different potential risks and hazards that employees and employers must be vigilant of. Here are some examples:

Factories:

- Exposure to hazardous chemicals and substances that can cause both short-term and long-term harm
- Use of heavy machinery that can lead to accidents and even amputations
- Inadequate ventilation leading to respiratory problems
- Noise pollution leading to permanent hearing loss
- Lack of proper ergonomic equipment leading to musculoskeletal disorders

Construction sites:

- Falls from heights due to uneven surfaces, ladders, and scaffolding
- Electrocution due to exposed wires and faulty electrical equipment
- Trench collapses and cave-ins leading to suffocation and burial
- Use of heavy machinery and vehicles leading to accidents
- Exposure to hazardous chemicals and substances

Offices:

Poor indoor air quality due to inadequate ventilation, leading to respiratory problems

- Inadequate ergonomic equipment, leading to musculoskeletal disorders
- Poor lighting leading to eye strain and headaches
- Stress and anxiety due to long working hours and high-pressure deadlines
- Fire hazards due to electrical equipment and overheating of office equipment

It is essential to implement proper safety protocols in these workplaces to reduce the risk of accidents and long-term health effects. Employers must prioritize the well-being of their employees and provide the necessary training, equipment, and precautions to ensure a safe and healthy workplace.

How Workplace Safety Can Affect Employee Morale, Productivity & Even Job Satisfaction:

Workplace safety is critically important for any business, not only for the safety of employees but also for the productivity and success of the company. The effects of workplace safety go beyond physical safety alone. A safe work environment affects employee morale, job satisfaction, and productivity, all of which directly or indirectly impact the success of the organization.

When employees perceive their safety is at risk or when safety protocols are not adhered to in the workplace, morale is affected. Employees might become anxious or fearful of injuries, leading to increased absenteeism, disengagement, and decreased work satisfaction. This negative attitude can spread throughout the workplace and even to customers, potentially leading to lower sales, loss of revenue, and a tarnished business reputation.

An unsafe work environment can, logically, lead to injuries, which could negatively affect an employee's health and well-being, leading to missed work or even disability. This can cause morale to spiral down, with missed paychecks or the possibility of job loss. Employees that feel their safety is not being prioritized can seek flexibility by looking for another job, unable to perform at their best because of the anxiety.

. . .

At the same time, workplace safety concerns can lead to lower productivity levels. Employees worried about their safety or about other unsafe conditions, are likely to fixate on these concerns and lose focus on the task in hand, leading to lower performance levels. When employees are concerned about safety, they cannot focus on their work, leading to a decline in quality and production levels.

A safe work environment is not only important for the physical safety of employees, but it also contributes to a positive work environment, higher employee morale, increased productivity, and job satisfaction. Employers who show a sincere commitment to workplace safety not only promote the welfare of their employees but also a positive work culture, which can enhance the organization's reputation and overall success.

Future Trends and Advancements in Workplace Safety:

As workplace safety continues to gain more importance globally, several new trends and advancements have emerged to reduce risks and prevent accidents, including innovative technologies and strategies. The future of workplace safety looks bright, and key developments to look out for include:

Emerging technologies and their role in workplace safety

Several emerging technologies are contributing to the safer workplace of tomorrow, including Artificial Intelligence (AI), the Internet of Things (IoT), and drones. With AI, businesses can analyze vast amounts of data to identify high-risk areas and take proactive measures to mitigate hazards. The IoT is also gaining significance in ensuring workplace safety, with sensors and wearables tracking vital signs and detecting potential hazards like gas leaks and machine malfunctions. Drones are also becoming increasingly important in the detection and prevention of workplace hazards, especially in the construction and manufacturing industries.

Improved training and support

Training and support have always been critical parts of workplace safety, but advancements in technology have made them more efficient and personalized. With virtual reality (VR) and augmented reality (AR) technologies, employees can learn about potential hazards and practice safety procedures in a virtual environment. This innovative way of training makes sure employees are adequately prepared to handle real-world situations, reducing the risks of accidents.

Greater emphasis on mental health

Several industries like healthcare, law enforcement, and social services involving high-stress jobs have recognized the importance of discussing mental health issues in the workplace. The COVID-19 pandemic has also caused a surge in mental health issues among employees. There is a growing emphasis on reducing job-related stress, improving work-life balance, and offering Employee Assistance Programs (EAPs) to support workers' mental well-being.

Collaboration between employers and employees

Another trend that will shape the future of workplace safety is increased collaboration between employers and employees. Employers are realizing the importance of involving employees in identifying and mitigating workplace hazards and soliciting their input in developing workplace safety procedures. This collaborative approach also creates a culture of safety where employees feel valued and are more likely to report potential hazards.

. . .

The future of workplace safety looks promising, with emerging technology, improved training and support, greater emphasis on mental health, and collaborative approaches between employers and employees shaping the landscape. With these trends, expectations are high that accidents and injuries will decrease, and employees will feel safer and more productive in their workplaces.

* * *

In our next chapter we explain your OH&S rights and responsibilities.

Chapter 3

Understanding Your Rights & Responsibilities

The Legal Framework of Occupational Health & Safety:

O H&S refers to the measures taken by employers to ensure a safe working environment for their employees. There are various laws and regulations that outline the legal framework of OH&S in most countries around the world. This legal framework protects workers from harm while they are at work. Understanding these laws and regulations is essential for both employers and employees.

The legal framework of OH&S consists of various laws and regulations that require employers to provide their employees with a safe working environment. These laws and regulations outline the responsibilities of both the employer and the employee in ensuring a safe work environment.

. . .

Employers are responsible for providing their employees with the necessary training, protective equipment, and facilities to make sure they are not exposed to any health or safety hazards while at work. Employers are also responsible for conducting risk assessments and taking measures to prevent accidents from occurring.

Employees, on the other hand, are required to comply with the policies and procedures established by their employers regarding OH&S. This includes following the safety guidelines, using protective equipment where necessary, and reporting any potential hazards or accidents to their employers.

The legal framework of OH&S also establishes the role of regulatory bodies responsible for enforcing these laws and regulations. These regulatory bodies make sure employers comply with the laws and regulations, and act against employers who fail to do so.

The legal framework of OH&S is essential for making sure employers provide their employees with a safe working environment. Employers must prioritize their employees' health and safety, and employees must follow the established policies and procedures. Helped by regulatory bodies, the framework makes sure employers adhere to the laws and regulations. Ultimately, a safe workplace benefits everyone involved.

The Responsibilities of Employers:

An employer must ensure that their employees are safe and healthy while they are at work. To do this, there are certain duties and obligations they must fulfill. These include:

   1. Providing necessary training: Employers are responsible for providing their employees with the necessary training to perform their jobs safely and effectively. This may include training on how to use equipment, how to handle hazardous materials, and how to respond in emergency situations.

2. Providing necessary equipment: Employers must ensure that their employees have the necessary equipment and tools to perform their jobs safely. This includes providing personal protective equipment (PPE) such as gloves, goggles, and hard hats, as well as making sure machinery and other equipment is up-to-date and functioning properly.

3. Maintaining a safe work environment: Employers must take steps to ensure that the workplace is free from dangers that could cause harm to employees. This may include removing hazards such as overhanging objects or exposed wiring, and making sure work areas are properly ventilated and well-lit.

4. Creating and implementing safety policies: Employers must create and implement safety policies that outline the steps that employees should take to stay safe on the job. These policies should be communicated clearly and regularly to all employees.

5. Responding to accidents or injuries: Employers must have a plan in place for responding to accidents or injuries that occur on the job. This may include providing first aid or emergency medical care and reporting the incident to the proper authorities.

. . .

Employers have a responsibility to ensure that their employees are safe and healthy while they are at work. By providing necessary training, equipment, and resources, maintaining a safe work environment, implementing safety policies, and responding to accidents or injuries, employers can fulfill these duties and obligations and create a safer workplace for everyone.

The Responsibilities of Employees:

As an employee, it is your responsibility to maintain a safe and healthy work environment not only for yourself but also for your colleagues. You must adhere to certain guidelines and protocols to ensure that everyone is protected from potential hazards and accidents. Here are some of the key responsibilities of employees that relate to maintaining a safe and healthy work environment:

1. Follow safety protocols: Different workplaces have different safety protocols that employees must follow to avoid accidents and injuries. These protocols may include wearing protective gear, properly storing equipment, using safe lifting techniques, avoiding dangerous behaviors, and many more. All employees must adhere to these protocols to ensure their own safety and that of others.

2. Report incidents and injuries: If you or any of your colleagues see an incident, accident, or injury in the workplace, it must be reported to the relevant authority. This could mean informing your manager or supervisor, reporting to the HR department, or contacting emergency services. Reporting such incidents is crucial to prevent future accidents and ensure medical attention is provided.

· · ·

3. Keep the work environment clean and organized: A clean and organized workplace creates a conducive environment that is easy to work in and reduces the chances of accidents. Employees should take responsibility for keeping their workstations, common areas, and shared equipment clean, tidy, and free of obstructions.

4. Use equipment and tools properly: When using equipment and tools, employees should follow the manufacturer's instructions and adhere to safety regulations to prevent accidents. Employees should avoid modifying the equipment or tools without permission, as it increases the risk of accidents.

5. Attend safety training sessions: Many workplaces provide safety training sessions to employees to help them understand the safety protocols, hazards, and preventive measures relevant in their specific work environment. Employees are expected to attend and participate in such sessions to increase their knowledge and awareness about workplace safety.

Employees play an essential role in ensuring a safe and healthy work environment. By following safety protocols, reporting incidents, keeping the environment clean and tidy, using equipment properly, and attending safety training sessions, employees can maintain a safe and healthy workplace for themselves and their colleagues.

The Importance of Reporting Incidents and Injuries:

Reporting incidents and injuries is crucial for maintaining a safe working environment. It not only benefits the individual involved but also helps to inform workplace policies and procedures for future prevention.

Personal Well-being: Reporting incidents and injuries can help make sure individuals receive the proper medical attention they need. Even minor accidents or incidents can result in long-term health issues if left untreated. Reporting incidents and injuries quickly can also help prevent any further damage and make sure the correct measures are taken to help promote a speedy recovery.

Workplace Policies and Procedures: Reporting incidents and injuries can help businesses and organizations identify potential hazards and risks within their workplace. By gathering information on incidents, they can put measures into practice to help prevent future accidents or incidents.

Reporting incidents can also help organizations identify areas of their workplace that need improvement. By identifying potential hazards and assessing the situation, organizations can identify and implement strategies to minimize risks and hazards in the workplace.

Reporting incidents and injuries is essential to safeguard personal well-being and to improve workplace policies and procedures. By reporting incidents and injuries, individuals can ensure they receive the proper medical attention they need, while businesses and organizations can identify potential hazards and put measures into practice to keep their employees safe.

The Consequences of Non-Compliance:

Non-compliance with OH&S regulations can have severe consequences for individuals and organizations. The following are some of the potential legal, financial, and reputational damage resulting from non-compliance:

Legal Consequences:

Failing to comply with health and safety regulations can lead to legal consequences such as fines, penalties, and legal suits. In the case of severe accidents, injuries, or death, negligence claims and criminal charges could be brought against the individual or organization responsible, leading to significant legal and financial costs.

Financial Consequences:

Non-compliance with OH&S regulations can result in substantial financial costs, ranging from fines and penalties to legal fees associated with defending against prosecution charges. In severe cases, loss of licenses, business closure, and increased insurance premiums may result, leading to significant financial losses.

Reputational Damage:

Non-compliance with OH&S regulations may harm an individual or company's reputation. The neglect of employees' safety and well-being can result in a damaged reputation that can take significant time and investment to recover. Negative press coverage, social media backlash, and negative word-of-mouth may lead potential clients to avoid doing business with the company and may further harm organizational growth and development.

Non-compliance with OH&S regulations can lead to difficult legal, financial, and reputational consequences. Failing to prioritize employee safety can be problematic, and non-compliance with laws and regulations can have serious consequences for organizations and individuals. To maintain a good reputation and avoid these consequences, it is essential to prioritize workplace safety and to comply with all relevant laws and regulations.

* * *

In our next chapter we explore the role of workplace culture in promoting safety.

Chapter 4

Workplace Culture And Safety: Understanding The Role Of Workplace Culture In Promoting Safety

I n the world of OH&S, workplace culture plays a crucial role in promoting safe behaviors and reducing risk to employees. Workplace culture refers to the shared beliefs, values, behaviors, and norms that shape the way people work together within an organization. When workplace culture focuses on and promotes safety, employees feel empowered to adopt safe behaviors and report unsafe conditions or incidents.

Communication is a crucial part of workplace culture that can affect safety. Open and regular communication channels between workers, supervisors, and management can foster a culture of collaboration and trust, enabling workers to identify and report potential hazards early on. In contrast, a lack of communication or ineffective communication can lead to confusion or misunderstandings, resulting in unsafe practices or incidents.

. . .

Leadership is another essential ingredient in promoting a safety culture. When leaders prioritize safety and lead by example in adopting safe practices, they set the tone for the entire organization. This also means investing resources in safety, training employees extensively on safety protocols, and recognizing and rewarding safe behavior. Leaders who focus on safety show their commitment to keeping employees safe, which builds trust, respect, and loyalty among workers.

Attitudes toward safety also play a crucial role in shaping workplace culture. If workers or management view safety as a burden, an unnecessary expense, or a hindrance to productivity, they may be less likely to focus on safety adequately. An organization that focuses on safety views it as an investment, recognizing that safe working conditions are essential for both employees' well-being and organizational success.

Workers who feel valued, respected, and safe tend to be more productive, more engaged, and more likely to stay with their employer. By prioritizing workplace culture and creating an environment that promotes safety, organizations can reap the benefits of a happy, healthy, and productive workforce. As such, prioritizing workplace culture and safety is not only the right thing to do for employees but also an essential part of organizational success.

* * *

In our next chapter we offer resources for support.

Chapter 5

Resources For Support

Incidents or injuries can happen to anyone at any time. When these incidents occur, it is essential that employees are aware of the resources available to them. Here is a list of resources for support that employees can turn to for help:

1. **Employee Assistance Programs (EAPs):** Many companies offer EAPs to their employees, which provide confidential counseling and support services. EAPs may also offer referrals to local support groups or legal professionals.

2. **Health Insurance:** Employees should review their health insurance policy to see what coverage is available for incidents or injuries. This may include coverage for medical treatment, mental health support, and rehabilitation.

. . .

3. **Support Groups:** Local support groups can offer emotional and practical support to employees following incidents or injuries. For example, a support group for individuals who have experienced workplace accidents can provide a safe space to share experiences, tips for coping with recovery, and advocacy resources.

4. **Legal Assistance:** Employees may need legal assistance if their injury or incident resulted from workplace negligence or misconduct. Resources such as workers' compensation lawyers or personal injury lawyers can help employees navigate their legal options.

5. **Employee Rights:** Employees should know their rights regarding incidents or injuries in the workplace, including their right to report unsafe working conditions or file a workers' compensation claim. They can consult with a labor law attorney to understand their rights.

Remember, seeking support resources is not a sign of weakness. It is a sign of strength to acknowledge when help is needed and to reach out for support.

* * *

In our next chapter we identify and assess workplace hazards.

Chapter 6

Identifying And Assessing Workplace Hazards

Techniques For Identifying Potential Workplace Hazards:

Here are techniques that can identify potential workplace hazards:

1. Perform a hazard assessment: This involves assessing the work environment and the tasks that employees perform to identify potential hazards.

2. Conduct workplace inspections: Regular inspections can help identify potential hazards and unsafe work practices.

3. Review incident reports: Reviewing incident reports can help to identify hazards and risks that may have been overlooked.

. . .

4. Analyze job tasks: Analyze the job tasks to identify potential hazards through job safety analysis (JSA), which is a technique used to break down a job task into steps and then identify potential hazards associated with each step.

5. Observe employees at work: Observing employees at work can help identify potential hazards and identify any unsafe work practices.

6. Conduct employee surveys: Employee surveys can provide valuable feedback on potential hazards in the workplace.

7. Review equipment maintenance and repair records: Regularly reviewing equipment maintenance and repair records will identify issues that require immediate attention and rectify hazards.

8. Consult with industry experts: Consult with industry experts such as safety consultants, engineers, and industry associations to identify potential workplace hazards.

By using these techniques, employers and employees can work together to identify and address potential workplace hazards, which can go a long way in reducing workplace accidents and injuries.

Different Types of Hazards That Can Be Present in A Workplace:

Hazards are present in almost every workplace, but the type and degree of hazard may vary depending on the nature of the job. The following are the different hazards that can be present in a workplace:

1. Physical hazards: These include hazards that can cause physical harm to a person. Examples include slippery floors, falling objects, sharp edges, electrocution, and excessive noise.

2. Chemical hazards: These include hazards that can be caused by exposure to toxic chemicals, such as asbestos, lead, benzene, and pesticides. Workers who work with such chemicals must follow Occupational Safety and Health Administration (OSHA) regulations to protect themselves from exposure.

3. Biological hazards: These hazards are caused by exposure to infectious agents such as viruses, bacteria, and fungi. Workers exposed to such agents risk contracting illnesses such as hepatitis, tuberculosis, and AIDS.

4. Ergonomic hazards: These hazards result from poor ergonomic design of the workplace, such as improper posture, repetitive motion, and lifting heavy objects. These hazards can cause musculoskeletal disorders such as back pain, tendinitis, and carpal tunnel syndrome.

. . .

5. Psychosocial hazards: These hazards arise from social interactions in the workplace such as bullying, harassment, and discrimination. They can lead to stress, anxiety, and depression.

Identifying hazards in the workplace is crucial in ensuring the safety and well-being of workers. Employers are required by law to identify, assess, and manage workplace hazards to minimize the risk of injury and illness.

Analysis Of the Likelihood and Severity of Each Identified Hazard:

Risk assessment matrices are tools used to evaluate the likelihood and severity of potential hazards. They typically consist of a table with the likelihood and severity of the hazard on each axis. The likelihood is usually measured on a scale of low to high, while severity can be measured on a scale from minor to catastrophic.

Once a hazard is identified, it is assessed in terms of its likelihood of occurrence and the potential severity of its consequences. This information is entered into the risk assessment matrix, which generates a risk score that indicates the level of risk associated with that hazard. Based on the risk score, the organization can decide whether to accept the risk, mitigate it, or avoid it altogether.

Hazards with a high likelihood and a high severity score are considered top priority and require immediate attention. Hazards with a high likelihood but a low severity score may require attention, but not as urgently as those with a high severity score. Hazards with a low likelihood and a low severity score are typically low priority and may require no action.

. . .

Overall, risk assessment matrices provide a structured and systematic approach to identify, evaluate, and focus on hazards. This lets organizations allocate resources effectively and make informed decisions to manage risk.

Strategies For Mitigating Hazards Once They Have Been Identified:

Once hazards have been identified, it is crucial to develop strategies for mitigating them to prevent accidents, injuries, and illness. The following are effective strategies for mitigating hazards:

1. Engineering Controls: These rely on physical changes to equipment, machinery, or processes to minimize hazards. Some examples include installing barriers or guards to separate workers from hazardous tasks or placing exhaust ventilation systems to remove hazardous substances from the air.

2. Administrative Controls: These involve changing work practices or policies to minimize exposure to hazards. Some examples include job rotation, training employees on safe work practices, and instituting strict procedures for handling hazardous materials.

3. Personal Protective Equipment (PPE): These are devices that are worn by employees to protect them from hazards, such as gloves, helmets, respirators, and safety glasses. PPE should be provided to employees based on the level of risk associated with their job tasks.

. . .

4. The Hierarchy of Controls: The hierarchy of controls is a systematic approach to mitigating hazards that recommends using engineering controls first, followed by administrative controls, and finally, personal protective equipment. The hierarchy of controls makes sure the most effective strategies are implemented to minimize risks to workers.

Mitigating hazards requires a combination of approaches, including engineering controls, administrative controls, and personal protective equipment. Employers should focus on the implementation of the hierarchy of controls to minimize risks to workers and promote a safe working environment.

The Importance of Ongoing Hazard Monitoring and Continuous Improvement Processes to Maintain a Safe Work Environment:

Once hazards have been identified, it is crucial to develop strategies for mitigating them to prevent accidents, injuries, and illness. The following are effective strategies for mitigating hazards:

1. Engineering Controls: These rely on physical changes to equipment, machinery, or processes to minimize hazards. Some examples include installing barriers or guards to separate workers from hazardous tasks or placing exhaust ventilation systems to remove hazardous substances from the air.

2. Administrative Controls: These involve changing work practices or policies to minimize exposure to hazards. Some examples include job rotation, training employees on safe work practices, and instituting strict procedures for handling hazardous materials.

. . .

3. Personal Protective Equipment (PPE): These are devices that are worn by employees to protect them from hazards, such as gloves, helmets, respirators, and safety glasses. PPE should be provided to employees based on the level of risk associated with their job tasks.

4. The Hierarchy of Controls: The hierarchy of controls is a systematic approach to mitigating hazards that recommends using engineering controls first, followed by administrative controls, and finally, personal protective equipment. The hierarchy of controls makes sure the most effective strategies are implemented to minimize risks to workers.

Mitigating hazards requires a combination of approaches, including engineering controls, administrative controls, and personal protective equipment. Employers should prioritize the implementation of the hierarchy of controls to minimize risks to workers and promote a safe working environment.

Examples Of Successful Hazard Identification and Mitigation Programs in Different Industries:

1. Aerospace Industry: NASA's Safety and Mission Assurance (SMA) Program has a robust hazard identification and mitigation process used across all its space missions. The program uses a hazard analysis process that identifies potential hazards and evaluates risks associated with them. Once these hazards are identified, mitigation strategies are developed and implemented to reduce risks to acceptable levels.

. . .

2. Pharmaceutical Industry: In the pharmaceutical industry, hazard identification and mitigation programs are required by regulatory bodies to ensure product safety. Companies like Pfizer have implemented robust pharmacovigilance programs that track for adverse effects of their drugs and take necessary actions to mitigate risks.

3. Oil and Gas Industry: The oil and gas industry is notorious for its potential hazards, which makes it important to have robust hazard identification and mitigation programs. Companies like Shell have implemented a Process Safety Management (PSM) program, which identifies hazards associated with their processes and develops strategies to mitigate them.

4. Construction Industry: The construction industry faces many hazards, which makes it important to have a strong hazard identification and mitigation program in place. Companies like Balfour Beatty have developed programs that identify potential hazards before construction begins and implement mitigation strategies to reduce risks.

5. Automotive Industry: The automotive industry places a strong emphasis on safety, which makes it important to have a robust hazard identification and mitigation program. Companies like General Motors have implemented a comprehensive safety program that identifies potential hazards associated with their products and puts measures into practice to mitigate risks.

6. Chemical Industry: The chemical industry is another industry notorious for its potential hazards, which makes it important to have a strong hazard identification and mitigation program. Companies like DuPont have implemented a Hazard Identification and Risk Management (HIRM) program, which identifies potential hazards associated with their products and develops strategies to mitigate them.

In our next chapter we introduce personal protective equipment.

Chapter 7

Personal Protective Equipment

Overview Of Personal Protective Equipment (PPE):

Personal Protective Equipment (PPE) refers to any equipment, clothing or device used to protect workers from hazards that may cause injury, illness, or death in the workplace. PPE is necessary in workplaces where hazards cannot be eliminated or controlled through engineering or administrative controls. This equipment acts as a barrier between the worker and the hazard. PPE can include a variety of equipment such as gloves, hardhats, respirators, safety glasses, face shields, protective clothing, and footwear.

Different types of PPE are designed to protect workers from specific hazards. For example, respirators protect workers from breathing in harmful particles or fumes, while safety glasses and goggles protect the eyes from flying debris. Hard hats are primarily designed to make sure a worker's head is protected from falling objects or electrical hazards.

. . .

Employers must ensure that the correct PPE is provided to workers exposed to hazards in the workplace. In addition, the employer must also train workers on how to properly use and maintain their PPE to make sure they are adequately protected. This will help to reduce the risk of injuries or illnesses associated with exposure to workplace hazards.

PPE is an essential tool for ensuring workplace safety, and it plays a crucial role in protecting workers from hazards. Employers must make sure PPE is properly selected, used, and maintained to protect workers from occupational injuries and illnesses.

Types Of PPE:

Personal Protective Equipment (PPE) is essential to ensure the safety and well-being of individuals working in hazardous environments. Different jobs require different types of PPE to provide adequate protection. In this section, we will discuss the different types of PPE and their uses:

1. Protective Clothing

Protective clothing includes coveralls, lab coats, gowns, aprons, and vests which protect the wearer from hazardous materials, chemicals, radiation, and flames. They are often made of specialized materials resistant to chemicals, flames, and other hazardous substances.

2. Helmets

Helmets protect the head from various physical risks such as falling objects, electrical hazards, and impacts. They can be made of plastic, fiberglass, or other materials.

3. Goggles

Goggles protect the eyes from chemical splashes, dust, and other airborne hazards. They are essential for industries such as mining, welding, and chemical processing.

4. Gloves

Gloves protect the hands from cuts, punctures, abrasions, and chemical exposure. Different gloves are available for different purposes, such as chemical-resistant gloves, heat-resistant gloves, and cut-resistant gloves.

5. Footwear

Footwear such as safety boots, shoes, and slip-resistant footwear provide protection against slips, trips, and falls, as well as exposure to hazardous substances.

The choice of PPE should be based on the hazards present in the work environment. Determine which PPE is required for each job task to ensure maximum protection for workers. Proper training should also be provided to make sure PPE is used correctly and maintained properly. Overall, using PPE is an essential practice to ensure worker safety and minimize the risk of injury or illness.

How To Use Different Types Of PPE:

. . .

Personal Protective Equipment or PPE is vital in safeguarding individuals against potential hazards in their working environment. However, it is important to note that different types of PPE require different usage protocols. Here is a guide on how to use different types of PPE:

1. Gloves – Gloves play an important role in protecting the hands from harmful substances and sharp objects. When wearing gloves, ensure they fit correctly and have no damage or tears. Before putting on gloves, wash your hands thoroughly to prevent contamination. Remember to remove gloves right after use and dispose of them properly.

2. Masks – Wearing a mask is essential to reduce the spread of airborne diseases or when working with hazardous materials. Choose the proper mask based on the type of work being done. Surgical masks should be worn with the blue side facing outwards, while respirator masks need to be fitted to ensure proper protection. Change masks regularly and dispose of them correctly.

3. Eye and Face Protection – Eye and face protection should be worn when working with hazardous materials or activities that could injure the eyes or face. Safety goggles or face shields provide adequate protection. Goggles should fit tightly against the face, with no gaps, and have anti-fogging properties. Face shields should be worn combined with goggles for maximum protection.

4. Footwear – Protective footwear is necessary for activities involving heavy or sharp materials or hazardous substances. Choose shoes that have steel toes and slip-resistant soles. Make sure footwear is well-fitted and that laces or straps are tight.

5. Protective Clothing – Protective clothing is required when working with hazardous substances or activities that could result in skin abrasions or cuts. This includes flame-retardant clothing, coveralls, and aprons. Protective clothing should be worn snugly, without being too tight or too loose.

Knowing how to use different types of PPE is vital to ensure safety in the workplace. Always use appropriate PPE for the job and follow usage protocols to ensure maximum protection. Regularly inspect and replace PPE if it becomes damaged or worn out. Remember - PPE only works if it is used correctly!

Maintenance & Inspection:

Proper maintenance and inspection of personal protective equipment (PPE) is essential to make sure it functions effectively and provides adequate protection to the wearer. Follow these guidelines to properly care for and maintain your PPE:

1. Cleaning: Clean PPE after each use to remove dirt, grime, and other contaminants. Use a mild detergent and warm water to clean hard hats, safety glasses, and earplugs. Use disinfectants to clean respirators and gloves. It is important to follow the manufacturer's guidelines for cleaning each piece of equipment.

. . .

2. Storage: Store PPE in a clean, dry place away from direct sunlight, chemicals, and other hazards. Use designated storage areas for each type of PPE to prevent damage and contamination.

3. Inspection: Regularly inspect PPE to make sure it is in good condition and functioning properly. Check for cracks, tears, or other signs of wear and tear. Inspect straps, buckles, and other fasteners to make sure they are secure and in good condition. If any damage is found, replace the PPE immediately.

4. Replace as necessary: Discard PPE damaged, worn out, or no longer provides adequate protection. Never try to repair or modify PPE yourself, as this may compromise its effectiveness.

5. Train employees: It is important to train employees in proper PPE maintenance and inspection procedures. This will make sure they are aware of the risks associated with improper maintenance and can take the necessary steps to protect themselves.

Proper maintenance and inspection of PPE is crucial to make sure it provides adequate protection to the wearer. Follow these guidelines to care for and maintain your PPE to ensure it is always in good condition and functioning effectively.

Employee Responsibilities & Training:

Using Personal Protective Equipment (PPE) is vital for ensuring workplace safety. While employers bear the primary responsibility for providing and maintaining PPE, employees must also take responsibility for their own safety. In this section, we will discuss the roles and responsibilities of both employers and employees in using PPE.

Employee Responsibilities

Employees are responsible for using PPE as directed by their employers. This includes attending training sessions on the proper use, care, and maintenance of PPE. Employees must also report any defects or damages to their PPE and seek replacement as necessary.

Employees must use PPE properly to protect themselves and their co-workers from injury or illness. They must use PPE in compliance with company policies and procedures and any relevant regulations. Employees should also communicate with their employers regarding any concerns about using PPE.

Training on PPE Use

Employers must provide their employees with proper training on how to use PPE effectively. Training should include instructions on how to wear, adjust, and remove PPE safely. Employees should also be trained in how to identify when PPE is necessary, how to inspect PPE for damage, and how to properly store and maintain PPE.

Employers should make training on PPE use a priority for new employees and provide frequent refresher training for existing employees. Training should be tailored to the specific PPE requirements of each employee's job.

. . .

Using PPE is vital for ensuring workplace safety. Employees must take responsibility for their own safety by properly using PPE and reporting any defects or damage. Employers must provide proper training on PPE use to ensure that employees are equipped to use PPE safely and effectively. By working together, employers and employees can create a safe and healthy workplace.

Legal Requirements:

Personal Protective Equipment (PPE) is an essential part of workplace safety. Employers have a legal obligation to provide their workers with PPE to protect them from potential hazards. Failure to comply with these regulations can result in serious consequences for the employer, including fines and legal action. This section summarizes the legal requirements regarding PPE in the workplace and the consequences of non-compliance.

Legislation

The Occupational Safety and Health Administration (OSHA) is the primary regulatory body responsible for setting standards regarding PPE in the workplace. OSHA mandates that employers provide PPE to their workers when there are potential hazards that cannot be eliminated through engineering or administrative controls.

OSHA standards require employers to assess the workplace for hazards, select appropriate PPE based on the degree of risk and worker needs, and provide training to workers on proper use, storage, and maintenance of PPE. OSHA standards also require the employer to replace damaged or worn-out PPE and make sure workers are using the PPE correctly.

Consequences of Non-Compliance

Employers who violate OSHA standards regarding PPE face serious consequences, including fines and legal action. Depending on the nature and severity of the violation, fines can range from hundreds to thousands of dollars. Employers who repeatedly violate OSHA standards face even higher fines and can be subject to criminal prosecution in severe cases.

Failure to provide PPE to workers can also cause injuries, illnesses, and even fatalities. In addition, workers who are injured due to a lack of PPE can file workers' compensation claims against their employer, which can be costly for the employer in terms of medical bills, lost productivity, and increased insurance rates.

Employers must comply with legal requirements regarding PPE in the workplace to ensure the safety of their workers and avoid serious consequences. Employers must assess hazards, select appropriate PPE, provide training, and replace damaged or worn-out PPE to comply with OSHA standards. Failure to comply with these regulations can result in fines, legal action and, most important, risk the safety and well-being of workers.

Choosing The Right PPE:

Personal Protective Equipment, or PPE, refers to any equipment or clothing specifically designed to protect the wearer from hazards and risks that may be present in their workplace or work environment. Selecting the right PPE is critical, as it greatly affects the safety and well-being of the wearer. Here are factors that need to be considered when choosing the right PPE:

Level of Protection Needed

The first consideration when selecting PPE is the level of protection required for the intended activity or work environment. Different hazards require different types of PPE. For example, eye and face protection may be necessary when working with chemicals, while hearing protection may be necessary in a noisy environment. It is important to identify all potential hazards and select the proper PPE to protect against them.

Comfort

Comfort is a major factor in choosing the right PPE. PPE that is uncomfortable or that doesn't fit properly can not only cause discomfort but can also reduce the effectiveness of the PPE. The PPE should fit properly and be compatible with other equipment or clothing that may be worn. It is important to try on PPE before buying it to ensure a good fit.

Cost

Cost is another important factor to consider when choosing PPE. While it is important to have the best protection available, cost also needs to be considered. Looking for PPE that provides a good balance between affordability and quality is key.

.   .   .

Functionality

PPE should not only provide protection but also be functional for the intended activity or work environment. For example, gloves should be flexible enough to allow for dexterity and movement when necessary. The PPE should also meet any specific industry standards or regulations.

Selecting the right PPE requires careful consideration of the level of protection needed comfort, cost, and functionality. Taking the time to choose the right PPE can greatly reduce the risks and hazards faced in the workplace, ensuring a safe and healthy work environment.

* * *

In our next chapter we introduce emergency preparedness.

Chapter 8

Emergency Preparedness

Understanding The Importance of Emergency Preparedness:

The unpredictability of emergencies can result in grave consequences if we are not prepared for them.

Examples of why proactive emergency planning is necessary:

- A sudden earthquake could cause buildings to collapse, trapping people inside, and without adequate planning, rescuers might not be able to do much to help.
- Torrential rainfall could cause flash floods with little warning, and people who are not equipped with their emergency kits might be stranded and at risk of exposure.

- In the case of a massive power outage, communication, transportation, and emergency services could be severely affected, leaving people cut off from help.

Having a specific emergency plan in place, along with a well-stocked emergency kit, can potentially save countless lives in any emergency. It's essential to be aware of the potential risks in your local area and prepare accordingly. By preparing before the emergency strikes, you will be much better equipped to deal with any situation that arises.

Knowing The Different Types of Emergencies:

Emergencies come in various forms, shapes, and sizes. It is important to know the types of emergencies that can happen so we can be well-prepared if they occur. Below are some of the most common emergencies:

1. Natural Disasters: Natural disasters can be devastating and unpredictable. These include earthquakes, floods, hurricanes, tornadoes, landslides, and wildfires.

2. Fires: Fires can occur due to various reasons such as electrical faults, gas leaks, cooking accidents, or smoking. They can spread quickly and cause serious damage and fatalities.

3. Medical Emergencies: These can range from injuries such as cuts, bruises, and broken bones to life-threatening illnesses like heart attacks, strokes, and severe allergic reactions.

. . .

4. Acts of Violence: These are undefined acts that can happen anytime, anywhere such as shootings, bombings, riots, and terrorism.

5. Environmental Emergencies: These can include contamination of water, air, and soil, as well as hazardous materials spills and releases.

6. Transportation Accidents: These happen during transportation such as plane crashes, train derailments, or car collisions.

Knowing the different types of emergencies can prepare us for the unexpected. It is important to have a plan in place and the necessary emergency supplies to deal with these situations. Being prepared can make all the difference between life and death.

Responding To Medical Emergencies:

Medical emergencies can happen at any time and knowing how to respond can save a life. Some common emergencies include heart attacks, seizures, choking, and strokes.

In the case of a heart attack, call 911 right away and perform CPR if the person is unresponsive. If someone is experiencing a seizure, make sure they are in a safe place and clear any objects around them to prevent injury. Do not hold them down or put anything in their mouth.

. . .

If someone is choking, perform the Heimlich maneuver by standing behind them, placing your fists above their navel, and giving quick upward thrusts. In cases of a stroke, remember the acronym FAST: Face drooping, Arm weakness, Speech difficulties, Time to call 911.

Being prepared for a medical emergency by taking a first aid or CPR class can also help you respond appropriately in critical situations. Remember to always focus on safety and call for professional medical help when needed.

Reacting To Natural Disasters:

Natural disasters can strike at any time, leaving destruction and devastation in their wake. It's important to be prepared and know how to react when disaster strikes. In this section, we will discuss some of the most common natural disasters and provide tips on how to respond.

Hurricanes: Hurricanes are powerful storms that can cause significant damage to homes and infrastructure. To prepare for a hurricane, it's important to create a disaster kit that includes food, water, and supplies to last at least 72 hours. If you live in an area prone to hurricanes, plan to evacuate your home if necessary and seek shelter in a designated safe zone.

Earthquakes: Earthquakes occur when there is a sudden release of energy in the Earth's crust, causing the ground to shake. If you are in an earthquake-prone area, it's important to have an emergency plan in place. This plan should include a communication system with your family and a disaster kit. During an earthquake, you should drop to the ground, take cover under a sturdy piece of furniture, and hold on until the shaking stops.

Tornadoes: Tornadoes are violent storms that can cause widespread damage. If a tornado has been spotted in your area, it's important to seek shelter immediately. If you are at home, head to a basement or interior room without windows. If you're in a car, abandon it and seek shelter in a sturdy building or ditch.

It's important to be prepared for natural disasters and know how to respond when they occur. Create a disaster kit, have an emergency plan, and know the safest places to seek shelter in your area. By taking these steps, you can protect yourself, your family, and your community when disaster strikes.

Responding to Fires:

Fires can happen to anyone, anywhere, and at any time. However, you can reduce the probability of having a fire by following simple tips.

First, avoid smoking indoors and never leave a burning cigarette unattended; it can quickly become a source of ignition. Also, always unplug appliances when not in use, and never overload extension cords. Be cautious when using heating equipment, such as space heaters, and ensure they are at least three feet away from combustible objects.

Despite taking precautions, fires may still occur. So, it is crucial to have a plan in case of a fire. Develop fire escape plans and practice them often with your family. Know where your exits are, and make sure they are accessible and not blocked by clutter. Also, make sure everyone in the house knows what to do when an alarm sounds.

Most important, have fire extinguishers readily available and know how to use them. Make sure they are inspected and maintained regularly. Never try to extinguish a fire if it is too large or if you are not confident in your ability to do so. In such cases, evacuate and call the fire department immediately.

Preventing fires requires adherence to simple tips, like avoiding smoking indoors, unplugging appliances, and being cautious with heating equipment. However, it's important to be prepared for the worst-case scenario by having a fire plan in place, knowing your exits, and having functioning fire extinguishers.

The Role of First Aid:

First aid is the provision of immediate care and support to injured or ill individuals. It is an important first response that can be the difference between life and death. First aid can be administered in various situations such as accidents, cardiac arrest, choking, bleeding, burns, fractures, and many more.

To administer first aid, one must be trained in basic techniques such as opening the airway, checking for breathing, stopping bleeding, and providing CPR or using an Automated External Defibrillator (AED). Having a first aid kit is also essential as it has the necessary supplies to handle minor injuries and emergencies.

· · ·

Knowing how to perform CPR or use an AED is crucial as it can help revive someone who has suffered cardiac arrest. In addition, choking can be a life-threatening situation, and knowing how to dislodge an obstructed airway could save a person's life.

Overall, first aid is a critical part in emergency response. Be prepared by having the necessary training and supplies to provide immediate care and support until further medical attention can be obtained.

Planning For Emergencies:

- Planning for emergencies is essential for every individual, family and organization. Emergencies can strike at any time, from natural disasters like earthquakes and hurricanes, to unexpected accidents or incidents.

- Being prepared includes having a plan in place for how to respond to emergencies. This plan should include identifying safe spaces, evacuation routes, and gathering emergency supplies.

- Stocking emergency kits is critical for any emergency plan. These kits should include a first aid kit, food and water, a flashlight, batteries, and any necessary medications. It is recommended to have at least a three-day supply of these resources for each person.

- Knowing when to evacuate is also crucial. Follow emergency alerts and listen to advice from authorities if evacuation is recommended. Have a backup plan in place, such as staying with friends or family, if you cannot return to your home or workplace immediately.

- Planning for emergencies is crucial, and everyone should take the steps to prepare themselves and their families. Being prepared can save lives and prevent further damage during an emergency. Remember to plan, stock up on emergency supplies, and know when to evacuate.

Ergonomics & Injury Prevention:

Understanding the Basics of Ergonomics: This section can introduce the fundamental principles of ergonomics, including proper posture, positioning, and movement during work-related activities.

Ergonomics is the science of designing tools, equipment, and work environments to fit the physical and mental capabilities of individuals. It involves understanding how the human body works and how it interacts with various tools and equipment used in workplace settings. Ergonomics tries to create a comfortable, efficient, and healthy work environment that reduces the risk of injury, illness, and fatigue.

Proper posture is one of the most important factors in ergonomics. Maintaining good posture while sitting or standing can help prevent muscular strain and reduce the risk of injury. To achieve proper posture, the back should be straight, the shoulders relaxed, and the feet flat on the ground. The computer screen should be at eye level to prevent neck strain, and the keyboard and mouse should be positioned within easy reach.

Positioning is another part of ergonomics. It involves adjusting the work environment to fit the worker's needs. For example, adjusting the height of a chair or using a footrest can help to maintain proper posture and promote good circulation. Proper positioning of tools, equipment, and work materials can also help reduce the risk of injury and fatigue.

Movement is also critical to ergonomics. Repetitive motions or staying in the same position for extended periods can lead to injury. Take frequent breaks and stretch sometimes to prevent strain and fatigue. Workers should also be educated on how to perform their work tasks with the least exertion, stress, and risk.

Ergonomics is concerned with designing work environments, tools, and equipment that are safe, comfortable, and efficient. Understanding the basics of ergonomics - proper posture, positioning, and movement - can help workers avoid injury, reduce stress, and increase productivity. By taking simple steps to improve the workplace environment, employers can create a safer, healthier, and productive work environment for their employees.

Common Causes of Musculoskeletal Injuries:

Musculoskeletal injuries are a common problem in the workplace, affecting workers in almost every industry. These injuries can occur due to a wide range of factors, including:

1. Repetitive Motions: Doing the same motions repeatedly, such as typing or making the same movement on an assembly line, can lead to strain injuries.

. . .

2. Awkward Postures: Holding an awkward or uncomfortable posture for an extended period can lead to muscle fatigue and strain.

3. Heavy Lifting: Lifting heavy objects, especially if done improperly, can cause injuries to the muscles, joints, and spine.

4. Ergonomic Issues: Poor ergonomics of a workspace, such as poorly designed chairs or workstations, can cause musculoskeletal disorders.

5. Lack of Training: Workers who are not properly trained in good body mechanics and safe lifting techniques are more prone to musculoskeletal injuries.

6. Age and Physical Condition: Older workers and those with pre-existing musculoskeletal conditions are more susceptible to injuries.

7. Prolonged Standing or Sitting: Standing or sitting for extended periods of time can cause muscle fatigue, poor circulation, and pain.

8. Stress and Fatigue: High levels of stress and fatigue can cause muscle tension and result in an increased risk of injuries.

By understanding these common causes of musculoskeletal injuries, employers can try to reduce the risk of injury and create a safer workplace. This can include ergonomic assessments, proper training, and putting policies into practice that encourage workers to take frequent breaks and practice good body mechanics.

Strategies For Preventing Injuries:

Injuries can occur at any time and can affect people of all ages and activity levels. Whether you are a professional athlete or someone who enjoys a leisurely stroll, it's important to take preventive measures to avoid injuries. Here are strategies that can help:

1. Warm up properly: Always take time to warm up before engaging in any physical activity. A proper warm-up can help increase blood flow to muscles, improve flexibility, and reduce the risk of injury.

2. Use proper equipment: Use proper equipment, such as helmets, gloves, padding, and shoes with good support, to ensure your safety during physical activities.

3. Listen to your body: Don't push too hard too fast. Listen to your body and know your limitations. If something hurts, stop or modify the activity to avoid injury.

4. Stay hydrated: Drink water before, during, and after physical activity. Dehydration can lead to muscle cramps and fatigue, which can increase the risk of injury.

. . .

5. Take breaks: Take frequent breaks during physical activity to give your body a chance to rest and recover. This is especially important if you're engaging in an activity for a long period.

6. Stretch: Incorporate stretching into your routine to improve flexibility and reduce the risk of injury. Focus on stretching the muscles you'll use the most during your activity.

7. Cool down: After physical activity, take time to cool down and stretch. This can help reduce stiffness and soreness in the muscles and prevent injury.

8. Get plenty of rest: Make sure you get enough rest and recovery time. Lack of sleep and rest can increase the risk of injury.

By following these strategies, you can reduce your risk of injury during physical activity and live a healthier, more active lifestyle.

Importance of Rest and Recovery:

Rest and recovery are two vital elements of physical health and well-being that often get overlooked in today's fast-paced society. Many people believe that working relentlessly for extended periods is a sign of strength or dedication, but the opposite is true, and neglecting rest is harmful to the body and mind.

The primary goal of rest and recovery is to let the body heal and restore itself after phase of intense physical activity or strain, which is a natural process. This relaxation time is when the body repairs damaged muscle fibers and replenishes depleted energy stores. Neglecting to rest and recover can lead to a wide range of negative consequences, from poor immune function to more severe problems like burnout, stress, or chronic disease.

Recovery is also essential for improving performance and building strength. When the body is allowed to recover, it becomes stronger and more resilient, leading to longer-term improvements in athletic or professional pursuits. Also, adequate rest has been linked to better sleep quality, improved mental health, and a reduced risk of injury.

It's critical to understand that recovery does not necessarily mean doing nothing. Active recovery, like stretching or a brief low-intensity workout, can also help the body recover from intense activities, depending on the severity of the workout. But complete rest is equally important sometimes and is recommended when the body is excessively strained, as in an injury or illness.

Rest, and recovery are crucial parts of physical health and well-being. It's essential to prioritize these activities and remember that they are not signs of laziness or weakness. Neglecting to rest and recover can lead to a wide range of negative consequences on your body, making it crucial to make adequate time for them.

Ergonomic Assessments:

As businesses continue to focus on the health and safety of their employees, ergonomic assessments have emerged as a critical tool in maintaining a safe and productive workplace. These assessments involve evaluating the physical environment of the workplace to identify potential hazards and putting measures into practice to reduce the risk of injury.

Ergonomic assessments are especially important for jobs that require repetitive motions, heavy lifting, or prolonged sitting. By identifying potential hazards early on, employers can take steps to minimize the risk of musculoskeletal disorders, such as carpal tunnel syndrome or back pain. In doing so, companies can not only protect their employees from injury but also improve their overall quality of life by preventing chronic pain and discomfort.

Another benefit of ergonomic assessments is that they can help optimize productivity in the workplace. When employees are working in a comfortable and safe environment, they are less likely to experience fatigue or pain, which can negatively affect their productivity. By putting ergonomic measures into practice such as adjustable workstations or anti-fatigue mats, businesses can help their employees work more efficiently and effectively.

Ergonomic assessments should be conducted regularly to ensure ongoing safety in the workplace. Employers should make sure that their assessments are carried out by trained professionals who understand the unique risks and demands of each job. By keeping up with these assessments, businesses can make sure they are providing the safest and most comfortable work environment possible for their employees.

Ergonomic assessments are a crucial part of maintaining a healthy and safe workplace. By identifying potential hazards and putting measures into practice to reduce the risk of injury, businesses can protect their employees from harm and increase productivity. Companies should prioritize these assessments as part of an ongoing commitment to employee health and safety.

Injury Management and Rehabilitation:

Injury management and rehabilitation are crucial parts in the recovery process for individuals who have experienced musculoskeletal injuries. Musculoskeletal injuries can result from various causes, including sports accidents, falls, and sudden impacts. Despite the cause, injury management and rehabilitation strategies aim to decrease pain, improve function, and help with a safe return to daily activities and sports participation.

The treatment options available to individuals who have experienced musculoskeletal injuries vary depending on the severity of the injury, the individual's medical history, and the specific needs of the patient. Physical therapy is often used as the first line of treatment to help with recovery from musculoskeletal injuries. Physical therapy can include exercises to strengthen the injured area and improve range of motion and manual therapy techniques to reduce pain and improve joint mobility.

In addition to physical therapy, medication may be prescribed to manage pain and inflammation associated with musculoskeletal injuries. Pain relievers may alleviate pain and discomfort, while anti-inflammatory drugs may reduce swelling in the affected area.

Surgery may also be necessary in cases of severe musculoskeletal injuries. Surgical intervention may have to repair broken bones, torn ligaments or tendons, or damaged joint cartilage. Following surgery, physical therapy and rehabilitation are necessary to promote healing and prevent further injury.

Injury management and rehabilitation are critical parts of the recovery process for individuals who have experienced musculoskeletal injuries. Treatment options vary depending on the severity of the injury, the individual's medical history, and the specific needs of the patient. Physical therapy, medication, and surgery are all potential treatment options for musculoskeletal injuries, and an individualized treatment plan facilitates a safe and successful rehabilitation.

Future Directions in Ergonomics & Injury Prevention:

As the field of ergonomics and injury prevention continues to evolve, advances in technology and research are shaping the future of workplace safety. Here are potential emerging trends and future developments in this field:

1. Wearable Technology: One of the latest trends in ergonomics is the use of wearable technology to enhance worker safety. Wearable devices can track workers' movements and provide real-time feedback on posture, fatigue levels, and ergonomic risk factors. These devices can be useful for workers in physically demanding jobs, such as construction workers, warehouse staff, and healthcare workers, as they can help prevent musculoskeletal injuries and improve workplace safety.

· · ·

2. Virtual Reality: The use of virtual reality (VR) technology in ergonomics and injury prevention is also gaining popularity. VR simulations can provide workers with a realistic experience of working in hazardous conditions or performing physically demanding tasks. This technology can help identify potential hazards in the workplace, letting employers make necessary improvements to prevent accidents and injuries.

3. Advanced Workplace Safety Protocols: Another key trend in ergonomics is the development of more advanced workplace safety protocols. These protocols identify and address ergonomic risk factors in the workplace, such as repetitive motions or awkward postures. By starting these protocols, employers can reduce the likelihood of workplace injuries and improve the overall health and well-being of their employees.

4. Healthcare Interventions: As the population ages, there is a growing need for healthcare interventions that focus on injury prevention and ergonomics. Many healthcare providers are implementing programs that teach older adults how to prevent falls and avoid injury in their daily lives. These interventions can be beneficial for older adults who may have physical limitations or chronic conditions that increase their risk of injury.

The future of ergonomics and injury prevention looks promising, with new technology and research helping to improve workplace safety and reduce the risk of injury. Employers who focus on implementing advanced safety protocols, wearable technology, and healthcare interventions will be better equipped to protect their workers and create a safer work environment.

* * *

In our next chapter we explore workplace violence and harassment.

Chapter 9

Workplace Violence & Harassment

Workplace Violence and Harassment – Definition & Types:

Workplace violence and harassment refer to any form of behavior that threatens or causes physical or psychological harm to an employee in the workplace. There are different types of violence and harassment that can occur in the workplace, and they include:

1. Physical Violence - This type of violence involves physical assault or aggression against an employee. It can include hitting, shoving, pushing, or physical attacks with a weapon.

2. Verbal Abuse - This type of violence involves threatening or intimidating language toward an employee. It can include shouting, name-calling, cursing, or making obscene gestures.

. . .

3. Sexual Harassment - This type of harassment involves unwanted sexual advances, requests for sexual favors, or any other sexual behavior that makes an employee uncomfortable.

4. Bullying - This harassment involves repeated aggressive behavior toward an employee. It can include verbal abuse, humiliation, or exclusion from work-related activities.

5. Psychological Harassment - This type of harassment involves behavior meant to create a hostile work environment for an employee. It can include intimidation, belittling, or spreading rumors.

It is important for employers to have policies in place to prevent workplace violence and harassment, and to ensure employees feel safe in their work environment.

Understanding The Causes and Effects of Workplace Violence & Harassment:

Workplace violence and harassment are serious issues that can have a significant impact on individuals and organizations. While there are many causes and effects of workplace violence and harassment, some of the most common include:

Causes:

1. Personality conflicts: personality differences or conflicts can escalate and lead to physical or verbal altercations.

. . .

2. Power imbalances: individuals who feel they lack power or control in their jobs may resort to violence or harassment to exert power over others.

3. Poor communication: misunderstandings or lack of communication channels between employees and employers can lead to frustration and eventually, conflict.

4. Workplace culture: a toxic work culture that tolerates or even encourages violent or harassing behavior can create an unsafe environment.

5. External factors: domestic issues or personal problems outside of work can spill over to the workplace.

Effects:

1. Physical injuries: workplace violence can cause physical injuries that range from minor bruises to major injuries and death.

2. Psychological distress: individuals who experience workplace violence or harassment may suffer from psychological distress, such as stress, anxiety, depression, and post-traumatic stress disorder (PTSD).

. . .

3. Reduced productivity: a toxic work environment can negatively affect employee morale, leading to decreased productivity and increased absenteeism.

4. Reputational damage: organizations that fail to prevent or address workplace violence and harassment can experience reputational harm and loss of public trust.

5. Legal consequences: employers who fail to prevent or address workplace violence and harassment can face legal consequences, including lawsuits, fines, and penalties.

Overall, workplace violence and harassment can have severe consequences for individuals and organizations, making it crucial to address and prevent these issues. Employers can try to create a safe and respectful workplace by putting policies and procedures into practice, providing training and education, and focusing on communication and transparency.

How To Recognize Warning Signs & Respond to Incidents:

Recognizing warning signs and responding to incidents can be crucial for your safety and well-being. Here are tips to help you:

1. Understand your environment: Be aware of your surroundings and try to identify potential hazards. Note the location of exits and any emergency equipment that may be available.

. . .

2. Trust your instincts: If something feels off or suspicious, it's probably best to trust your gut instincts and take precautions. It's always better to be safe than sorry.

3. Keep an eye out for warning signs: Some potential warning signs to watch for include an escalating argument or confrontation, aggressive behavior, or someone acting paranoid or erratic.

4. Act: If you see warning signs, don't be afraid to take action. This could mean alerting someone in authority, contacting emergency services, or leaving the area.

5. Stay aware and prepared: Being aware of your surroundings and staying prepared with emergency supplies can help you respond quickly and effectively in the event of an incident.

By being aware of your surroundings, trusting your instincts, and acting, when necessary, you can help keep yourself and others safe in potentially dangerous situations.

The Importance of Documentation & Reporting Incidents of Violence or Harassment:

Documentation and reporting incidents of violence or harassment is imperative in maintaining a safe and secure working environment. It is essential to keep a record of such incidents as they help in identifying patterns, determining the root cause, and taking corrective measures to prevent future incidents.

. . .

Documentation serves as a valuable tool for legal and internal purposes. It enables individuals and organizations to gather and present evidence. This evidence can be used for various purposes such as further investigation, disciplinary action, legal proceedings, or even to improve training and awareness programs.

In addition to legal and internal purposes, documenting and reporting incidents of violence or harassment also helps in creating a culture of accountability and transparency. It sends a clear message that the organization takes such incidents seriously and is committed to providing a safe and healthy work environment for its employees.

Documentation and reporting also help with communication between the parties involved. It provides an opportunity for the victim to express their concerns, feelings, and experiences, and lets the management respond in a proactive and empathetic manner.

Documentation and reporting incidents of violence or harassment is crucial for creating a safe and secure working environment. It not only helps with legal proceedings and internal investigations but also fosters accountability, transparency, and communication within the organization. So every organization must establish a robust documentation and reporting system to ensure the safety and well-being of its employees.

Guidelines For Preventing and Addressing Workplace Violence & Harassment:

1. Develop and put clear policies and procedures into practice for preventing and addressing workplace violence and harassment.

· · ·

2. Provide regular training to all employees on identifying and reporting incidents of workplace violence and harassment.

3. Encourage an open-door policy where employees feel comfortable reporting incidents without fear of retaliation.

4. Investigate all incidents of violence or harassment in a timely and thorough manner, and take appropriate disciplinary action against perpetrators.

5. Provide support to employees who have experienced or witnessed workplace violence or harassment, including counseling services and access to legal resources.

Resources And Support Available for Employees Who Experience Workplace Violence or Harassment:

Here are resources and support available for employees who experience workplace violence or harassment.

1. Employee Assistance Program (EAP): Many workplaces have an EAP that offers confidential counseling and support services to employees who experience workplace violence or harassment.

2. HR Department: The Human Resource Department is responsible for ensuring a safe and healthy workplace environment for all employees. They can provide guidance on the reporting process and help with filing a complaint.

. . .

3. Union Representation: If the employee is a member of a union, they have access to union resources and support, including representation in the reporting process and support in the form of counseling.

4. Government Agencies: There are various government agencies, such as the Equal Employment Opportunity Commission (EEOC), that provide resources and support for employees who experience workplace violence or harassment. These agencies investigate complaints and provide legal recourse when necessary.

5. Legal Representation: Employees who experience workplace violence or harassment have the right to legal representation. Attorneys can provide guidance on filing a complaint, pursuing legal action, and helping with securing compensation.

1. **Employee Support Groups:** Many workplaces have support groups or Employee Resource Groups (ERGs) that focus on support for employees who experience workplace violence or harassment. These groups provide a safe space for employees to share their experiences, receive emotional support, and advocate for change.

2. **Police Support:** In severe cases, employees may require the help of the police. Employees can go to the nearest police station or call the emergency number to report the incident.

It is essential that employees who face workplace violence or harassment have access to support and resources. Employers must create a safe and supportive workplace environment for their employees.

Mental Health in the Workplace:

Mental health is a critical part of an employee's overall well-being, and it can have a profound impact on their productivity and job satisfaction. When employees are struggling with mental health issues, it can lead to decreased focus, energy, and motivation, which can negatively affect their work performance. Also, persistent stress and anxiety can lead to burnout, which can result in employee turnover, reduced productivity, and increased absenteeism.

Employers must focus on the mental health of their employees, as it is closely linked to their overall well-being and job satisfaction. By providing support and resources for mental health concerns, employers can reduce stress and promote a positive work environment. This can lead to increased productivity, employee retention, and overall job satisfaction.

Mental health concerns can have a significant impact on the physical health of employees, which can further impact productivity and well-being. Stress, anxiety, and burnout can lead to physical health issues, such as high blood pressure, heart disease, and even depression.

Investing in mental health initiatives for employees can lead to a positive work culture, increased productivity, and reduced employee turnover rates. Employers who focus on mental health and well-being in their workplaces are more likely to attract and keep top talent, as employees are more likely to feel valued and supported.

Prioritizing mental health in the workplace is crucial for employee productivity, job satisfaction, and overall well-being. Employers must invest in mental health initiatives to support their employees, which can lead to a positive work culture, improved physical and mental health, and increased job satisfaction.

Signs Of Common Mental Health Issues:

Anxiety:

- Constant worrying and feeling anxious
- Panic attacks
- Trouble sleeping
- Physical symptoms such as trembling, sweating, and nausea
- Avoiding certain situations or places
- -Irritability

Depression:

- Feeling sad or hopeless
- Lack of interest in activities
- Fatigue or loss of energy
- Difficulty sleeping or oversleeping
- Changes in appetite
- Trouble concentrating

- **Burnout:**

- Feeling exhausted
- Decreased productivity
- Feeling cynical or negative
- Irritability or anger
- Lack of motivation
- Difficulty concentrating or focusing

Strategies For Promoting Positive Mental Health in The Workplace:

Promoting positive mental health in the workplace is an important goal for any organization. A healthy workforce can improve productivity, reduce absenteeism, and create a more positive work environment. Here are strategies for promoting positive mental health in the workplace:

1. Employee recognition programs: Recognizing employees for their hard work and achievements can boost their self-esteem and motivation. Implementing a recognition program can encourage employees to meet their goals and feel valued in the workplace.

2. Flexible work arrangements: Offering flexible work arrangements such as telecommuting, flexible hours, and job sharing can reduce stress and improve work-life balance. This can help employees avoid burnout and improve their mental health.

3. Stress management training: Providing stress management training to employees can help them recognize the signs of stress and learn effective coping strategies. This can improve their resilience and reduce the impact of stress on their mental health.

. . .

4. Open communication: Encouraging open communication and creating a safe space for employees to discuss their mental health can reduce stigma and increase awareness. This can help employees seek help when needed and reduce the risk of mental health issues going unnoticed.

5. Wellness programs: Offering wellness programs such as yoga classes, meditation sessions, and nutrition workshops can improve employees' physical and mental health. This can reduce the risk of chronic diseases and improve overall well-being.

By implementing these strategies, organizations can promote positive mental health in the workplace and create a happier, healthier, and more productive workforce.

The Role of Managers & Colleagues in Supporting Employees with Mental Health Issues:

The role of managers and colleagues in supporting employees with mental health issues cannot be overstated. These individuals play a crucial role in creating a safe and supportive work environment for employees struggling with mental illness.

Managers, in particular, play a critical role in supporting employees with mental health issues. This includes identifying signs of distress, creating a culture of wellness, and providing resources and support for employees in need. Managers can also take steps to reduce stigma surrounding mental illness by openly discussing the importance of mental health and encouraging employees to seek help when needed.

. . .

Colleagues also have an important role to play in supporting employees with mental health issues. This includes being aware of signs of distress, listening non-judgmentally, and offering support and encouragement. Colleagues can also help to reduce stigma by openly discussing mental health and sharing their own experiences.

Ultimately, the role of managers and colleagues in supporting employees with mental health issues is to create a safe and supportive work environment that promotes wellness and reduces stigma. By working together, these individuals can help to improve the mental health and well-being of employees, leading to increased job satisfaction, productivity, and overall quality of life.

Resources For Employees and Employers to Access Mental Health Support:

Mental health is a crucial part of overall well-being, and employees and employers can benefit from access to mental health resources. Here are resources individuals can use to access mental health support:

1. **Employee Assistance Programs (EAP):** Many organizations offer EAPs as part of their employee benefits package. These programs offer free and confidential counseling and support to employees and their families. An EAP can assist with personal issues such as depression, anxiety, relationship problems, substance abuse, and financial or legal concerns.

2. **Counseling Services:** Many licensed therapists and counselors offer individual and group counseling services for mental health issues. These services can be accessed through insurance

providers or by seeking private providers or community-based organizations. Many employers also provide access to mental health services through their health insurance plans.

3. Crisis Hotlines: Many organizations provide crisis hotlines that are staffed with trained counselors available 24/7 to individuals in distress. These hotlines are free and confidential, and can provide support for a range of issues, including mental health crises, abuse, and suicidal thoughts.

4. Community Resources: Many local nonprofits, mental health clinics, and community organizations offer mental health programs and services. These resources can include support groups, counseling, educational materials, and referrals to other mental health resources.

Overall, it is important for employers and employees to focus on mental health and seek resources to maintain their well-being. Mental health support is available, and those who seek it are more likely to maintain positive mental health outcomes.

The Stigma Associated with Mental Health Issues and The Importance of Creating a Safe & Supportive Workplace Culture:

Mental health has been a topic of concern for individuals and businesses worldwide. Despite the growing awareness and advocacy campaigns, mental health issues are still plagued by a sense of stigma and shame. This stigma clouds discussions and hinders affected individuals from seeking help, resulting in increased anxiety and psychiatric disorders.

. . .

Employers are uniquely positioned to help combat this stigma by creating safe and supportive workplace cultures that encourage employees to seek help and support when needed. This means fostering an open and honest dialogue about mental health issues, focusing on access to mental health resources, and leading by example. Managers must take the responsibility to educate themselves and their teams about the mental health challenges, the importance of seeking help, and how to recognize signs of distress in co-workers.

Creating a safe, supportive, and non-judgmental workplace culture for employees struggling with mental health issues will result in many benefits. Employees will be less stressed, more productive, and more likely to stay in their jobs over the long term. Companies will benefit from reduced healthcare costs, increased employee satisfaction, and a more positive brand reputation.

The fight against the stigma of mental health is more critical now than ever before. It is time for businesses and individuals to break down the fears and misconceptions around mental health to create an inclusive and supportive workplace culture for all. It is only by doing this that we can build a better and healthier work environment for everyone.

* * *

In our next chapter we explore the effects of workplace culture and providing a safe and healthy environment.

Chapter 10

Workplace Culture

Workplace culture is an essential part of any successful organization and plays a significant role in employee engagement and satisfaction.

Workplace culture refers to the shared values, beliefs, attitudes, and behaviors that shape the work environment and affect the way employees interact with each other and the way work is carried out. A positive workplace culture creates a sense of community and fosters collaboration, open communication, and mutual respect among employees. This promotes a sense of belonging and helps with employee engagement, which leads to better job satisfaction, productivity, and employee retention.

A workplace culture that values diversity and inclusivity promotes creativity and innovation by bringing together a variety of perspectives and ideas. A culture of respect and trust leads to fewer conflicts and more effective problem-solving. A workplace culture that focuses on work-life balance and employee well-being reduces employee burnout and turnover.

However, creating and maintaining a positive workplace culture is not something that can be achieved overnight. It requires a deliberate and continuous effort from management and employees. This includes taking feedback from employees and making changes to improve workplace culture, recognizing, and rewarding employees who exemplify the desired behaviors and values, providing training and development opportunities, and promoting open communication and transparency.

Workplace culture is crucial to the success of any organization. A positive culture promotes employee engagement, satisfaction, and retention, leading to better productivity, innovation, and overall organizational performance. It requires continuous attention and effort, but the benefits of a healthy workplace culture are well worth it.

A Positive Workplace Culture Creates a Safe, Healthy, And Innovative Work Environment That Fosters Team Collaboration & Employee Motivation:

When employees feel valued and respected in the workplace, they are more likely to have higher levels of job satisfaction, which leads to better productivity and performance. A positive workplace culture supports this by emphasizing open communication, collaboration, and mutual support among co-workers. This encourages employees to feel connected and motivated to work together toward a common goal.

. . .

A positive workplace culture promotes a safe and healthy environment by focusing on the physical and mental well-being of employees. This can include offering wellness programs, providing support for mental health, and implementing safety protocols to prevent accidents and injuries. Employees who feel secure and healthy at work are more likely to feel satisfied with their jobs and perform their best.

A positive workplace culture fosters a culture of innovation, where employees are encouraged to think outside the box, share ideas, and experiment with new approaches to their work. This environment enables organizations to stay ahead of the curve by continually improving and adapting to changing circumstances. It also helps employees grow and develop their skills, leading to a more engaged and empowered workforce.

Creating and maintaining a positive workplace culture is essential for organizations to thrive. It promotes a safe, healthy, and innovative work environment that fosters team collaboration and employee motivation. Ultimately, companies that focus on workplace culture are more likely to attract and keep top talent, leading to long-term growth and success.

A Toxic Workplace Culture Can Negatively Affect Employees and Their Productivity, Leading to Increased Absenteeism, Turnover & Diminished Workplace Satisfaction:

Toxic workplace culture can have a detrimental impact on the overall psyche of employees. Working in a negative environment can take a toll on an individual's mental health, leading to increased stress, anxiety, and depression. This can negatively affect their productivity and job satisfaction.

Employees who find themselves in a toxic environment often experience increased absenteeism as they may come up with excuses to avoid coming to work. This may lead to reduced productivity and missed deadlines, ultimately affecting the quality of work produced.

A toxic culture can also lead to high turnover rates as employees may feel like they have no choice but to leave the organization in search of a better work environment. This is an expensive and demotivating process for the organization as they will need to dedicate time and resources to hiring and training new employees.

Overall, toxic culture can have a major impact on the overall health and well-being of employees, which can lead to negative effects on the organization's productivity, revenue, and success. So, it is crucial for organizations to actively work on promoting a healthy, inclusive, and positive workplace culture.

Staying Safe & Healthy:

Understanding the concept of self-care and its importance in maintaining overall health and well-being.

Self-care refers to the practice of taking care of oneself to promote and maintain overall health and well-being. This includes activities that enhance physical, emotional, and mental health. The concept of self-care involves being mindful of one's own needs, focusing on them, and taking active steps to meet them.

. . .

Self-care is important in maintaining physical health as it includes activities such as healthy eating, regular exercise, and adequate sleep. These activities help to keep the body functioning optimally, prevent illness, and promote longevity. Also, self-care plays an important role in emotional and mental health. It involves engaging in activities that promote relaxation and stress reduction, such as meditation, deep breathing, and spending time in nature. Taking care of oneself emotionally and mentally allows for greater emotional resilience, better stress management, and an overall sense of well-being.

It is important to recognize that self-care is not a luxury, but a necessity. Regular self-care practices promote happiness, health, and resilience, helping individuals better manage daily stressors, foster positive relationships, and enjoy a more fulfilling life. Engaging in self-care activities can also prevent burnout and mental exhaustion, which can contribute to physical and emotional health problems over time.

Self-care is an essential element of overall health and well-being. By prioritizing self-care practices, individuals can promote physical, emotional, and mental health and lead happier, healthier lives.

The Role of Regular Physical Activity and Exercise in Reducing The Risk Of Chronic Diseases Such As Obesity, Type 2 Diabetes & Hypertension:

Regular physical activity and exercise are essential for maintaining good health and reducing the risk of chronic diseases such as obesity, type 2 diabetes, and hypertension. These conditions are known as non-communicable diseases, and they are a significant contributor to the global burden of disease.

. . .

Obesity is a growing problem worldwide and is linked to many chronic diseases, including diabetes and hypertension. Regular physical activity and exercise can help manage weight by burning excess calories, increasing muscle mass, and reducing body fat.

Type 2 diabetes is a metabolic disorder characterized by high blood sugar levels resulting from the body's inability to produce or use insulin effectively. Exercise helps to regulate blood sugar levels by increasing insulin sensitivity, reducing insulin resistance, and improving glucose uptake by muscles.

Hypertension, or high blood pressure, is a major risk factor for heart disease, stroke, and kidney failure. Exercise helps to lower blood pressure by enhancing the elasticity of blood vessels, improving blood flow, and reducing the workload on the heart.

Regular physical activity and exercise also have other health benefits, including reducing the risk of certain types of cancer, improving bone health, and boosting mental health and cognitive function.

Regular physical activity and exercise are crucial for reducing the risk of chronic diseases such as obesity, type 2 diabetes, and hypertension. Adding moderate-intensity physical activity to daily routines has a significant impact on health outcomes and should be encouraged for all individuals.

The Importance of Eating a Balanced and Nutrient-Rich Diet to Promote Good Health, Prevent Chronic Diseases & Boost Immune Function:

Eating a balanced and nutrient-rich diet is crucial to maintaining good health and preventing chronic diseases. Many chronic diseases such as diabetes, heart disease, and cancer are rooted in poor diet and lifestyle choices. A balanced diet consisting of plenty of fruits, vegetables, whole grains, lean protein, and healthy fats can help prevent these diseases and reduce the risk of developing other illnesses.

In addition, eating a balanced diet with a variety of nutrients can help boost immune function, making you less susceptible to infections and illnesses. Nutrients such as vitamins A, C, E, and D, as well as zinc, iron, and protein, are all essential for immune health. By consuming a diet rich in these nutrients, you can help to support your immune system, making sure you stay healthy and strong.

Overall, the importance of a balanced and nutrient-rich diet cannot be understated. By making healthy choices and consuming a variety of foods, you can help to promote good health, prevent chronic diseases, and support strong immune function. So the next time you sit down to eat, remember the importance of making healthy choices that will benefit both your body and your mind in the long run.

Strategies For Managing Stress and Achieving Work-Life Balance to Reduce The Risk Of Burnout & Associated Health Problems:

- **Prioritize and delegate**: Make a list of all your tasks and prioritize them according to their importance. Delegate non-essential tasks to others if possible.
- **Time management:** Efficient use of time is crucial. Schedule breaks, allot time for specific tasks, and stick to a routine.
- **Self-care:** Prioritize self-care activities such as exercise, healthy eating, and relaxation techniques like meditation or yoga. Get enough sleep to restore energy and reduce stress levels.
- **Communication:** Maintain open communication with colleagues, managers, and family to ensure everyone knows their roles, and you can communicate your needs, and douse feelings of overwhelm.
- **Set boundaries:** Set clear boundaries between work and personal life. Avoid working long hours or bringing work home, deep friendships within your workspace might be very important but it is important to also get fresh perspectives from other avenues.
- **Manage expectations:** Manage expectations from yourself and others. Be realistic about what you can achieve and don't put too much pressure on yourself.
- **Seek support:** Seek support from family, friends, or even professional counseling if needed to help cope with stress and burnout.

Tips For Maintaining Good Sleep Hygiene and Getting Adequate Rest To Improve Overall Health & Well-Being:

- **Stick to a consistent sleep schedule:** Try to go to bed and wake up at the same time every day, including on weekends, to regulate your body's internal clock and establish a consistent sleep-wake cycle.

- **Create a relaxing bedtime routine:** Develop a calming routine that signals to your body that it's time to wind down for sleep. This could include taking a warm bath, reading a book, or practicing relaxation techniques such as meditation or deep breathing.

- **Limit screen time before bed:** The blue light emitted by electronic devices can disrupt your body's production of the sleep hormone melatonin, making it harder to fall asleep. Avoid using screens for at least an hour before bedtime.

- **Make your sleep environment conducive to rest**: Keep your bedroom cool, dark, and quiet, and invest in a comfortable mattress and pillows. Use blackout curtains or an eye mask if necessary to block out light, and earplugs or a white noise machine to muffle any noise.

- **Avoid stimulants and heavy meals before bedtime: Consuming** caffeine, nicotine, or alcohol too close to bedtime can interfere with sleep quality. Similarly, eating a heavy or spicy meal late at night can cause discomfort and make it harder to fall asleep. Try to finish meals and avoid stimulating substances at least 2-3 hours before bed.

Best Practices for Preventing Infectious Diseases and Minimizing the Risk of Exposure In Different Settings, Including At Home, In The Workplace & While Traveling:

Here are best practices for preventing infectious diseases and reducing the risk of exposure in different settings:

• • •

At home:

- Wash your hands often with soap and water for at least 20 seconds or use a hand sanitizer with at least 60% alcohol.
- Cover your mouth and nose with a tissue or your elbow when you cough or sneeze.
- Clean and disinfect often touched surfaces, such as doorknobs, countertops, and light switches, daily.
- Avoid close contact with people who are sick.
- Wear a mask when you are around people who do not live with you or when you are in a public place.
- Boost your immune system by eating a healthy and balanced diet, getting enough sleep, and managing stress.

In the workplace:
F

- ollow the guidelines provided by your employer, such as wearing a mask, practicing physical distancing, and getting vaccinated.
- Stay home if you are sick and inform your supervisor or manager.
- Wash your hands often with soap and water for at least 20 seconds or use hand sanitizer with at least 60% alcohol.
- Avoid touching your face, especially your eyes, nose, and mouth.
- Clean and disinfect your workstation and other frequently touched surfaces.

- Try to reduce face-to-face contact with co-workers and use virtual communication tools, such as email, chat, or video conferencing.

While traveling:

- Research the COVID-19 situation and entry restrictions of your destination before you go.
- Check if you need to get vaccinated or tested before or after your trip.
- Pack enough masks, hand sanitizer, and disinfecting wipes.
- Avoid crowded places and close contact with people who are sick.
- Wash your hands often with soap and water for at least 20 seconds or use a hand sanitizer with at least 60% alcohol.
- Follow the local guidelines and regulations, such as wearing a mask, practicing physical distancing, or quarantining upon arrival.

The Importance of Regular Health Screenings and Check-Ups to Catch Potential Health Problems Early & Maintain Optimal Health Throughout Life:

As we age, our bodies undergo various changes that can affect our overall health and well-being. Regular health screenings and check-ups play a crucial role in maintaining optimal health throughout life. These exams are designed to catch potential health problems early on and prevent them from becoming more serious conditions.

. . .

For example, many chronic illnesses such as heart disease, cancer, and diabetes can be prevented or effectively managed through early detection and treatment. Health screenings such as blood pressure tests, cholesterol tests, and mammograms are essential for detecting these conditions before they become problematic.

Another benefit of regular health screenings is that they let you establish a relationship with a primary care physician who can help you manage your health. This can be especially important if you have a family history of certain health conditions or if a chronic health condition requires ongoing care.

Regular check-ups can help you stay on top of your overall health and well-being. Your doctor can provide you with important information about healthy lifestyle choices, such as eating a balanced diet, getting enough exercise, and avoiding tobacco and alcohol.

Regular health screenings and check-ups are essential for maintaining ideal health throughout life. These exams let us catch potential health problems early on, establish a relationship with a primary care physician, and stay on top of our overall health and well-being. So, schedule your next health screening or check-up today, and take control of your health!

* * *

In the next chapter we explore your right to refuse work.

Chapter 11

Work Refusal

Introduction:

Definition of OH&S Work Refusal:

The act of an employee withholding their labor due to a reasonable belief that their work environment is unsafe or poses a danger to their health and well-being.

Reasons for Work Refusal: Employees May Refuse Work Due to a Variety of Reasons, Such As Inadequate Training or Equipment, Hazardous Materials or Substances, or Unsafe Working Conditions.

Importance of Work Refusal Procedure:

Legal Framework:

Relevant OH&S Legislation:

Terms of OH&S legislation will vary from one jurisdiction to another. You would be well advised to research the applicable legislation for your location.

Legal Protections for Employees: OH&S Legislation in Most Jurisdictions Protect Employees Who Refuse Work Due to Safety Concerns from Retaliation or Disciplinary Action by Employers.

Workers' Rights & Responsibilities:

Workers may refuse work that puts them at risk of physical harm or illness.

Responsibilities:

1. To understand the legal and moral framework surrounding work refusal: outlining the legal obligations of employers and employees, and the ethical considerations of refusing to work.

2. To understand the reasons for work refusal: exploring the reasons why an employee may refuse to perform a certain task or duty, such as safety concerns, harassment, discrimination, and other workplace issues.

3. To understand how to navigate the process of work refusal: how workers can go about effectively communicating their concerns to their employer, and how to escalate their complaints if necessary.

4. To understand protection for employees who refuse work: knowing the types of protection available to employees who refuse to perform work because of safety concerns or other related reasons.

5. Understanding Employer obligations when employees refuse work: knowing the steps that employers must take when an employee refuses to perform work, including risk assessments, investigations, and communication with the employee.

6. Understanding the consequences of work refusal: understanding the potential consequences of refusing to perform work, such as disciplinary action, termination, or legal action.

7. Balancing responsibilities with workplace safety: understanding the importance of finding a balance between an employee's responsibilities and the duty to have a safe work environment and providing tips for employees and employers to achieve this balance.

. . .

Employer Obligations:

Employers have a duty to provide a healthy and safe work environment for their employees and to address any concerns related to workplace safety promptly and effectively.

When to Refuse Work:

Conditions that Justify Work Refusal:

1. Unsafe working conditions that put employees in immediate danger can justify work refusal. This includes hazardous materials, unsafe equipment, or lack of safety protocols.

2. Lack of protective equipment or clothing necessary for the job is also justifiable as work refusal. Employees have the right to a safe working environment.

3. Discrimination, harassment or bullying from co-workers, supervisors or customers can be grounds for work refusal. Employees have the right to a work environment free of harassment.

4. Violation of labor laws or unethical practices can justify work refusal. This includes non-payment of wages, excessive overtime, or discrimination based on race, gender or religion.

. . .

5. Medical conditions, which make work difficult or impossible, can justify work refusal. This includes physical or mental disabilities or conditions.

Types of Hazards and Risks:

1. Biological hazards: exposure to infectious agents, such as bacteria, viruses, fungi, and parasites. Workers at risk include healthcare providers, laboratory technicians, and agricultural workers.

2. Chemical hazards: exposure to harmful substances, such as solvents, pesticides, and acids. Workers at risk include chemical workers, painters, and laboratory technicians.

3. Physical hazards: exposure to physical stressors, such as noise, vibration, radiation, and extreme temperatures. Workers at risk include miners, construction workers, and airport ground staff.

4. Ergonomic hazards: exposure to repetitive motions, awkward postures, and heavy lifting. Workers at risk include office workers, assembly line workers, and healthcare providers.

5. Psychosocial hazards: exposure to stressful working conditions, such as work-related violence, harassment, and bullying. Workers at risk include teachers, social workers, and customer service representatives.

Each hazard can pose various risks to workers' health and safety, depending on the nature of the work and exposure level.

Work Refusal Process:

Reporting the Hazardous Condition:

If you encounter a hazardous condition in the workplace, it is important to report it immediately. Refusing to work until the condition is addressed is a way to protect yourself and others from potential harm.

1. Notify Your Supervisor: As soon as you observe a hazardous condition, inform your supervisor or the designated authority figure about the problem. Provide details about the hazard, including its location and nature.

2. Document the Hazard: Take photos or videos of the hazardous condition if possible. This will serve as evidence that the condition exists and will help create awareness about the situation.

3. Ask for an Inspection: Ask for an inspection by relevant health and safety experts or authorized staff. This may be your Joint Occupational Health & Safety committee which would include a representative from the workers and the employer.

4. Wait for Response: After notifying your supervisor and requesting an inspection, it is important to wait for their response. Employers must address any hazardous conditions in the workplace. If they do not respond promptly or if they refuse to address the issue, you may need to escalate the matter to a higher authority or contact a regulatory body.

. . .

5. Refuse to Work: If the hazardous condition is severe and immediate action is required, you may need to refuse to work until the condition is addressed. Be sure to follow proper work refusal protocol and notify your supervisor in writing about your decision. Do not return to work until the hazardous condition is resolved.

6. Investigate the Incident: After the hazardous condition is addressed and resolved, make sure a thorough investigation of the incident is conducted. This will help prevent future incidents and keep the workplace safe for employees.

Remember that workers may refuse work that poses serious health and safety risks. By reporting hazards and refusing to work until they are addressed, employees can help create a safer work environment.

Escalation Process: (What could happen if the work refusal is not resolved to the employee's satisfaction.)

The escalation process for an OH&S workplace work refusal generally follows these steps if the issue is unresolved:

1. Step One: Informal Discussion - The first step is to informally discuss the issue with the worker, the supervisor, and the OH&S representative to understand why the worker is refusing to work.

2. Step Two: Investigation - The second step is for the supervisor and the OH&S worker representative to investigate the worker's work refusal thoroughly. This includes an assessment of the work area and work process to determine whether there are hazards.

3. Step Three: Conflict Resolution - If the investigation identifies hazards, the supervisor and the OH&S worker representative must resolve the issue with conflict resolution strategies such as mediation or facilitation.

4. Step Four: Formal Work Refusal Process - If the issue remains unresolved, the worker must submit a written work refusal to the supervisor with supporting evidence, such as photos or videos of the hazards. The supervisor then investigates and files a formal report. A joint health and safety committee (JHSC) or a health and safety representative reviews the report.

5. Step Five: Arbitration – If the issue is still not resolved, the parties may seek arbitration to resolve disputes arising in the application of workplace laws or contractual provisions.

6. Step Six: Legal Action - If arbitration fails, the worker may take legal action. This includes filing a complaint with the OH&S agency of the jurisdiction or seeking legal action through the court system.

Overall, the escalation process for an OH&S workplace work refusal, if the issue is unresolved, provides a systematic process for addressing and resolving workplace hazards that may affect the worker's health and safety at work.

Case Studies and Examples of Work Refusal Incidents and Their Resolution Under OH&S Legislation:

Case Study 1: Refusal to Work Due to Unsafe Conditions

In 2018, workers at a construction site in Sydney refused to work due to unsafe conditions. The workers noticed that several pillars supporting the building structure were not secured to the ground properly, which posed a high risk of collapse. The workers raised their concerns to the site supervisor, but he dismissed their worries and pushed them to continue working.

The workers then exercised their right to refuse work and contacted the Work Health and Safety (WHS) regulator. The regulator conducted a site inspection and confirmed that the workers' concerns were valid. The regulator issued a prohibition notice, halting all work at the site until the structural issues were resolved.

Because of the incident, the site supervisor and the construction company were fined for breaching OH&S legislation, and improvements were made to make sure workers were aware of their rights to refuse unsafe work.

Case Study 2: Refusal to Work Due to Bullying

In 2019, a healthcare worker at a hospital in Adelaide refused to work with a colleague who had been consistently bullying her. The worker had raised her concerns with her supervisor, but no action was taken to address the issue.

The worker then exercised her right to refuse work and reported the bullying to the WHS regulator. The regulator investigated the incident and found that the hospital had failed to provide a safe work environment, as required under OH&S legislation.

Following the investigation, the hospital implemented measures to prevent workplace bullying, including staff training and the appointment of a dedicated bullying contact officer. The worker was also provided with support to overcome the emotional distress caused by the bullying.

Case Study 3: Refusal to Work Due to COVID-19 Risks

During the COVID-19 pandemic in 2020, workers at a manufacturing plant in Melbourne refused to work due to concerns about the lack of COVID-19 safety measures in place. The workers reported that there was a lack of social distancing, no provision of personal protective equipment, and insufficient hand hygiene facilities.

The workers exercised their right to refuse work and reported the issues to the WHS regulator. The regulator inspected the plant and found that the employer had failed to provide a safe work environment in line with the COVID-19 guidelines.

. . .

The employer was ordered to put measures into practice to reduce the risks of COVID-19 transmission, including social distancing measures, provision of personal protective equipment, and improved hand hygiene facilities. The employer was also fined for breaching OH&S legislation.

These case studies highlight the importance of workers' rights to refuse unsafe work under OH&S legislation. Employers must provide a safe work environment and put measures into practice to address any hazards or risks that may arise. When workers feel that their safety is compromised, they have the right to stop work and raise their concerns to the WHS regulator for investigation and remedial action.

Sample Letter Of OH&S Related Work Refusal to Supervisor:

[Your name and position]
    [Date]

[Employer's name and address]
    [Supervisor's name]

Dear [Supervisor],

I am writing this letter to inform you that I have to refuse the work assigned to me for reasons of health and safety under the Occupational Health and Safety (OH&S) Act.

As you know, OH&S is the responsibility of the employer and the employees, and both parties must work together to ensure a safe and healthy working environment. Unfortunately, I believe that the work assigned to me poses an immediate danger to my health, safety, and life.

[Provide specific details about why you have to refuse the work, such as hazardous materials, unsafe equipment, inadequate training, lack of personal protective equipment or facilities, excessive workload, and other hazards.]

I have taken reasonable steps to report my concerns to you, but they have not been resolved. Therefore, I have no other option but to refuse the work until the situation is remedied.

I understand that work refusal can disrupt production and cause inconvenience to you and the organization. However, I hope you understand that my primary concern is my safety and that of my colleagues, and I cannot compromise that under any circumstances.

In accordance with the OH&S Act, I am requesting that an investigation be conducted promptly to address my concerns and determine the appropriate corrective action. I am also requesting that I be given other work that is safe and suitable for my skills and abilities while the investigation is ongoing.

Please be assured that I will continue to fulfill my responsibilities as an employee and cooperate with the investigation to the best of my abilities.

. . .

Sincerely,

[Your name and signature]

Conclusion

Did you make it to the end of the book?

I'll admit it can be a dry subject if you haven't been introduced to OH&S matters before. The best way to move forward is to consider this book as an ongoing reference resource.

As situations arise at work remember what you have learned and your eyes open to potential risks and hazards. Don't be surprised if you see complacency toward safety hazards from older workers or those working at the worksite for a while. If a manager doesn't promote safe working conditions, it may be passed on to the workers.

My hope is this book has sparked an interest in you and you seek further education and training in OH&S.

The field of OH&S needs more passionate, knowledgeable, and experienced leaders. Don't let your age and lack of experience prevent you from becoming more experienced and advocating on behalf of your fellow workers. We all had to start somewhere.

Take care... please!

Rae A. Stonehouse

Additional Resources:

Note that this is not an exhaustive list and there may be other valuable resources available in these regions.

North America:
Occupational Safety and Health Administration (OSHA): https://www.osha.gov/

Canadian Centre for Occupational Health and Safety (CCOHS): https://www.ccohs.ca/

National Institute for Occupational Safety and Health (NIOSH): https://www.cdc.gov/niosh/index.htm

Great Britain:

Health and Safety Executive (HSE): https://www.hse.gov.uk/

Institution of Occupational Safety and Health (IOSH): https://www.iosh.com/

Additional Resources:

New Zealand/Australia:

WorkSafe New Zealand: https://worksafe.govt.nz/

SafeWork Australia: https://www.safeworkaustralia.gov.au/

About the Author

Rae A. Stonehouse is a Canadian born author & speaker.

His professional career as a Registered Nurse working predominantly in psychiatry/mental health, spanned four decades.

Rae has embraced the principal of CANI (Constant and Never-ending Improvement) as promoted by thought leaders such as Tony Robbins and brings that philosophy to each of his publications and presentations.

Rae has dedicated the latter segment of his journey through life to overcoming his personal

inhibitions. As a 29+ year member of Toastmasters International he has systematically built his self-confidance and communicating ability.

He is passionate about sharing his lessons with his readers and listeners.

His publications thus far are of the self-help, self-improvement genre and systematically offer valuable sage advice on a specific topic.

His writing style can be described as being conversational. As an author Rae strives to have a one-to-one conversation with each of his readers, very much like having your own personal self-development coach.

Rae is known for having a wry sense of humor that features in his publications. To learn more about Rae A. Stonehouse, **visit The Wonderful World of Rae Stonehouse** at https://raestonehouse.com

Facebook: **https://www.facebook.com/raestonehouse.aws**

Twitter: https://twitter.com/raestonehouse

Also By Rae A. Stonehouse

Visit https://liveforexcellence.store/ for a selection of personal/professional self-development books by Rae A. Stonehouse.

If you have found this book to be helpful, please leave us a warm review wherever you purchased it.

www.ingramcontent.com/pod-product-compliance
Lightning Source LLC
Chambersburg PA
CBHW071203120626
46546CB00006B/2389